READING TOGETHER

A Reading/Activities Text for Students of
English as a Second Language

READING TOGETHER

A Reading/Activities Text
for Students of
English as a Second Language

KARL KRAHNKE
Colorado State University

NEW YORK   ST. MARTIN'S PRESS

Editor: Kathleen Keller
Managing editor: Patricia Mansfield
Project editor: Cheryl Friedman
Production associate: Katherine Battiste
Text design: Leon Bolognese & Associates, Inc.
Graphics: The Clarinda Company
Cover design: Judy Forster
Cover photo: Michael Zide

Library of Congress Catalog Card Number: 89–63912

For information, write:
St. Martin's Press, Inc.
175 Fifth Avenue
New York, NY 10010

ISBN: 0-312-01259-4

ACKNOWLEDGMENTS

Roger Caras, "We Must Find Alternatives to Animals in Research," *Newsweek,* December 26, 1988, p. 55. Reprinted by permission of the author.

Charles Coble, Dale Rice, Kenneth Walla, and Elain Murray, *Prentice Hall Earth Science,* Englewood Cliffs, New Jersey, pp. 239–242, 246–249, 264–269.

Claire Martin, "The Greatest Trainer on Earth," by Claire Martin, *Denver Post,* October 1, 1989, pp. D1, D7.

Jane McCabe, "Is a Lab Rat's Fate More Poignant Than a Child's?" *Newsweek,* December 26, 1988, p. 55. Reprinted by permission of the author.

John Merrill and Harold Fisher, *The World's Great Dailies,* 1980. Hastings House Publishers, New York, NY.

Martin Tennesen, "Myth of the Monster." Copyright 1989 by the National Wildlife Federation. Reprinted from October/November 1989 issue of *National Wildlife.*

To the Instructor

Reading Together is a reading and activities text for low intermediate students of English as a Second Language who are at a high-school or higher educational level. The book includes the following distinctive features:

- multiple readings on a similar topic
- longer readings than are typical in texts for this level of student
- many meaning-based activities that focus on text comprehension rather than reading skills, grammar, or vocabulary
- a large proportion of cooperative group learning activities

APPROACH

Reading Together comes out of teaching experience that has shown that reading for meaning is the best way to learn how to read, and that this process is facilitated when readers can use what they already know to help comprehend a text and when they can work together in understanding a text and applying knowledge from it. The book is also based on the idea that even lower-level readers can read relatively long texts in English and that reading such texts contributes both to the development of reading skills and of language acquisition in general.

DESIGN

The book is divided into seven chapters. Each chapter is devoted to one general topic and includes a variety of readings and activities that are related to the topic. The chapters share a similar format and contain similar, but not identical, types of activities. The final chapter differs from the previous six in that the readings are all taken from published sources with little or no adaptation. The activities in the final chapter are also more research-oriented.

ADVANTAGES

There are several advantages to the approach represented by this text. First, students are exposed to vocabulary repeatedly and in a variety of topic-related contexts. Vocabulary is not pre-taught, in isolation, but presented in a meaningful environment that encourages mature and productive meaning-discovery strategies and the unconscious acquisition of vocabulary.

Second, learners experience a variety of writing styles and points of view on a given topic. The styles of the readings included in the text are, of course, limited somewhat by the need to emphasize standard written English, but there is still variety in rhetorical type, informational content, and point of view.

Third, because the readings are focused on topics that students already know something about and need to take account of in their everyday lives, the readings are both interesting and comprehensible to students. The efficiency of the reading process is improved, and in this way the learning process is also made more efficient.

Fourth, by focusing in some of the activities on information and meaning rather than on language skills, *Reading Together* encourages the unconscious language acquisition process, since this process occurs more readily when learners concentrate on content rather than on the form of expression. A focus on information also emphasizes the uses of reading rather than the means by which reading is done; it makes the learning process more purposeful.

Fifth, and most important, through the use of group and pair activities the students are required to work with other students toward comprehension. Language acquisition and reading ability are made easier through this interaction with other learners. Many of the activities could be done individually and, in some cases, are activities that are traditionally done individually; however, by encouraging cooperative learning, a very different approach to comprehension and learning emerges, in which students share problems, needs, and resources, and negotiate solutions. Much more learning time is available to each student and the learning that goes on is usually more effective. In addition, since cooperative and group learning is increasingly common in secondary schools and universities in the United States, using the techniques in this text will help prepare students for group work in other academic environments.

An Instructor's Manual provides more detailed information to instructors about how best to use the book and how to implement specific activities.

ACKNOWLEDGMENTS

I would like to thank the following reviewers who provided useful comments on the many drafts of this text: Cathy Day, Eastern Michigan University; Irene Frankl, City University of New York; Charles Gillon, University of Tennessee at Martin; Lynn Goldstein, Monterey Institute of International Study; Shirley Oster, Bowling Green State University; Muriel Quintin, University of Hartford; Amy Sales, Boston University; May Shih, San Francisco State University; Sandra Silberstein, University of Washington; Margaret Steffenson, Illinois State University; and Frederica Stoller, Northern Arizona University.

Thanks are due to my wife, Keiko, for toleration and inspiration. Thanks are also due to the many people who helped shape the ideas and content reflected in the book: the teachers of the Institute for Intercultural Learning in Seattle; Maria Parish-Johnson; the staff of Colorado State University's Intensive English Program; Kathleen Keller, Cheryl Friedman, and Huntley Funsten of St. Martin's Press; and Susan Anker, formerly of St. Martin's Press.

Karl Krahnke

To the Student

This book will help you learn English. If you read what is in the book and do the activities, you will learn a lot of English, a lot about reading, and you will become a better language learner.

You will read a lot in this book and you will read in different ways. Sometimes the book will ask you to read slowly and carefully and to try to understand most of what you read. At other times you will be asked to read quickly and to get only a general idea of what is in the reading. What is important is that you *understand the information and ideas* in what you read.

You already know a lot about the subjects in this book. You know about education, food, marriage, and money, and the other subjects. You will learn new things as you read the book. As you read, think about what you already know. Many of the activities and exercises in the book will ask you to use what you already know. From what you already know about the subject, think of questions before and as you read to help you understand and learn more.

Many of the activities in the book ask you to work with other students. If you work with other students, you will learn from them and they will learn from you. Other students often know something about a subject that you do not. They can help you understand. Sometimes you know something about a subject that they do not and you can help them understand. Talking together will improve your English and help you learn what is in this book. As you work together, do not just listen to other students. Tell them what you know and ask them questions.

If you are going to be a good reader, you have to read a lot more than is in this book. Reading a lot is one of the best ways you can learn English. Be sure to keep a Reading Journal as you work on this book, and write about all of the reading that you do in your Reading Journal.

Chapter 5
TYING THE KNOT 126

Introduction 127
Vocabulary Introduction 127
Outside Reading 128
Information Gathering 129

SHORT READING 130

  Marriage Records 130
  Questions 131
  Fill-in-the-Blank 131

LONG READING 1 132

  Prereading Activity 132
  I Married the Same Woman Twice 133
  Questions 134
  Completion 134
  Information Identification 135
  Comparison 136
  Vocabulary Exercise 136

LONG READING 2 138

  Prereading Activity 138
  Marriage International 139
  Did You Think Of It? 140
  Giving Advice 141
  Information Identification 141
  Vocabulary Exercise 142

LONG READING 3 143

  Prereading Activity 143
  Rice, Rings, and Rituals 143
  Questions 144
  Completion 144
  Paraphrase 145
  Guessing 146
  Vocabulary Exercise 147
  Crossword Puzzle 148

Chapter Review 149
Writing or Speaking Summary 150
Reading Journal 151

Chapter 6
ANIMALS AND US 152

Introduction 153
Vocabulary Introduction 153
Outside Reading 155
Information Focusing 156

SHORT READING 157

    Exotic Animals and American Farms 157
    Questions 158
    Fill-in-the-Blank 158

LONG READING 1 159

    Prereading Activity 159
    The Myth of the Monster 161
    Questions 162
    Completion 163
    New Information 164
    Interview 164
    Vocabulary Exercise 164

LONG READING 2 166

    Prereading Activity 166
    The Greatest Trainer on Earth! 167
    Questions 169
    Comparison 169
    Summarizing 170
    Vocabulary Exercise 171

LONG READING 3 172

    Animal Rights, Human Wrongs? 172
    Prereading Activity 173
    Is a Lab Rat's Fate More Important Than a Child's? 174
    We Must Find Alternatives to Animals in Research 176
    Comparison 178
    Reasons and Opinions 178

Chapter Review 180
Writing or Speaking Summary 182
Reading Journal 183

Chapter 7
WATER AND US 184

Introduction 185
Outside Reading 186
Information Gathering 186

SHORT READING   187

>   Prereading Activity   187
>   *Water*   187
>   Questions   188

LONG READING 1   189

>   Prereading Activity   189
>   *Fresh Water on the Earth's Surface*   190
>   Questions   194
>   Fill-in-the-Blank   195
>   Applying the Text   196
>   Definitions   196
>   Using Information   197
>   Preparing a Report   197

LONG READING 2   198

>   Prereading Activity   198
>   *Oceans of the World*   199
>   Questions   203
>   Summary Writing   204
>   Comprehension Questions   204
>   Applying the Text   205
>   Extending the Text   206
>   Definitions   206

LONG READING 3   206

>   Prereading Activity   206
>   *Cities Athirst*   207
>   Questions   208
>   Comprehension Questions   208
>   Summary Writing   210
>   Vocabulary Exercise   211
>   Applying the Text   211

Chapter Review   212
Research Activity   213
Reading Journal   214

INDEX   217

READING TOGETHER

A Reading/Activities Text for Students of English as a Second Language

Chapter

1

GETTING
AN EDUCATION

Training is teaching how to do. Education is teaching how to learn how to do.
—Anonymous Educator

INTRODUCTION

This chapter is about education. At the top of this page is a definition of education. Do you think it is a good definition? Does the writer of this definition think that training is more difficult or that education is more difficult?

Working with a partner, think of three examples of training and three examples of education. Compare your examples with the examples thought of by other students. As a class, decide which is the best example of training and which is the best example of education.

VOCABULARY INTRODUCTION

Below are some words that are related to the subject of education. Work with a group of students in the class and see if you know what these words mean. If you do not know, ask other students, ask your instructor, or look in a dictionary to find out what they mean. Write the definition of each word you did not know on the blank lines at the top of page 4.

class	education	secondary
classroom	examination	subject
college	grade	university
course	graduate	
desk	intelligent	

DEFINITIONS OF WORDS YOU DID NOT KNOW:

1. _____

2. _____

3. _____

4. _____

5. _____

6. _____

7. _____

8. _____

Working with other students in your group, write on the lines below ten other words that are related to education. When you are finished, you or your instructor can write the words that the class thought of on the blackboard.

_____   _____   _____

_____   _____   _____

_____   _____   _____

_____

Write on the lines below any word written on the blackboard that you are not sure you know the meaning of.

_____   _____   _____

_____   _____   _____

_____   _____   _____

Review these words as you complete this chapter.

OUTSIDE READING

You should read other things written in English while you are studying this chapter. Reading other material about education will help you to understand this chapter better. Encyclopedias are a good source of basic information about education in different countries. Magazines often have articles about education. Most colleges and universities in English-speaking countries have catalogs that describe the university and its program. In the United States there are also guidebooks to colleges and universities that contain information on many schools. All of these can be good reading.

Take a few minutes in class and suggest outside readings about education and where to find them. Write on the lines below some good suggestions that you hear.

_____

_____

_____

_____

_____

Be sure to write about your outside reading in your Reading Journal. Suggestions for the Journal can be found at the end of this chapter.

INFORMATION GATHERING

Write your answers to the following questions in the space provided. When you are finished, your instructor will list each student's answers on the blackboard. Working in groups or as a class, count the answers. Then write the results of what you found out about the class.

1. How many years have you gone to school?

Your answer: _____

The student in class who has gone
to school the longest: Number of years _____

The student in class who has gone
to school the shortest: Number of years _____

2. How many different schools have you gone to?

Your answer: _____

(Continued at top of next page)

The student in class who has gone
to the most schools: Number of schools _____

The student in class who has gone
to the fewest schools: Number of schools _____

3. Do you like to go to school?

You: yes   no

Other students in class:
Number answering yes _____

Number answering no _____

4. Do you prefer a male teacher or a female?

You: male   female

Other students in class:
Number preferring a male _____

Number preferring a female _____

5. What is your favorite subject in school?

You: _____

What subject did most of the students in the class like best? _____

6. Do you plan to go to a university? Are you studying at a university now? Have
you gone to a university in the past?

You: _____

How many other students answered yes to any of the questions? _____

7. What do you want to do after you finish school? Or, what work are you
doing now?

You: _____

Five answers from other students in the class:

1. _____

2. _____

3. _____

4. _____

5. _____

S H O R T   R E A D I N G

PREREADING ACTIVITY

Read the following questions. When you are sure you understand the questions, read the passage that follows them carefully. It should take you five or ten minutes. After you have read the passage, answer the questions. (The questions are repeated after the reading.)

1. According to the reading, what are basic skills?
2. What have schools been teaching instead of basic skills?
3. In the opinion of many people, what is the result of the schools' failure to teach basic skills?
4. What have universities had to do to make up for students' lack of basic skills?
5. Is there another explanation for lower college entrance scores than the one given in the reading?
6. What do you think was the reason that schools were not teaching basic skills?

Back to Basics

Many Americans want their public education system to go back to teaching young people the basic subjects of English literature and composition, mathematics, and science. For two decades, the U.S. educational system has been offering courses in different subjects such as music, art, cooking, personal money management, and filmmaking. Many people believe that this has led to a lack of attention to the basic skills of writing, calculating, and thinking. 1

During the same twenty years, students' scores on college entrance examinations have been falling, and colleges have been complaining that the students coming to colleges and universities are not as well prepared as they were before. Universities have begun to teach more remedial courses in the basic skills to bring incoming students up to a level where they can do regular university work. University administrators, employers, and many parents are asking the public schools to return to a system with more required courses and fewer optional courses. 2

There are others, of course, who argue that today's students are just as   **3**
well-prepared for college as the students of twenty years ago were, and that tests
do not measure the kind of learning that students have been getting. They argue
that today's students are better prepared to live and work in the modern world
than students were before. This second view is not very common, however, and
there is now a popular, back-to-basics movement in education in the United
States. Many educators hope that this renewed emphasis on basic skills will both
prepare students to succeed in universities and prepare them to live in the
modern world.

QUESTIONS

Now write your answers to the questions from the beginning of the reading. You
may work in pairs if your instructor asks you to. Look back at the reading to check your
answers.

1. According to the reading, what are basic skills?

_____

2. What have schools been teaching instead of basic skills?

_____

3. In the opinion of many people, what is the result of the schools' failure to teach
basic skills?

_____

4. What have universities had to do to make up for students' lack of basic skills?

_____

5. Is there another explanation for lower college entrance scores than the one
given in the reading?

_____

6. What do you think was the reason that schools were not teaching basic skills?

_____

FILL-IN-THE-BLANK

Working with another student, fill in the blanks in the following passage. For
many of the blanks, more than one answer will be possible or correct, but put only

one word in each blank. Look carefully at the sentences that come before and after the blank to be sure that the word you choose has meaning in both the sentence and the paragraph and that the form of the word is correct for that sentence. Discuss with your partner any differences in the words you choose, your understanding of the sentences, and your reasons for choosing certain words. The purpose of the exercise is to find as many words that can fit in the blanks as possible.

When you and your partner have finished, your instructor will ask you to compare your answers with the answers that your classmates gave. Your instructor may ask you to write your words on the blackboard. Be ready to explain why you chose a word and what the word means. Also be ready to change your answer if other students found a better word. Write other good answers that you hear below the ones that you gave.

Going to School

For some of us, going to school is the most natural and normal activity in the

world. We became _____ when we were young, and some of us are still
                        (1)

students now. _____ means different things to different people, however.
                    (2)

For some, education means going to a college or _____, and getting a(n)
                                                        (3)

_____ from a university means getting a good _____ and
        (4)   (5)

an important social position. For others, education simply means learning how to

_____ and write.
        (6)

The majority of the people in the world still cannot read or _____; they
                                                                    (7)

are illiterate. For these people, education means _____ the basic skills of
                                                            (8)

reading, writing, and _____.
                            (9)

Education is also different in different countries. In some, education is mostly

free. The _____ pays the cost of education. In other countries
                (10)

_____ must pay, and often it is only the children of _____
        (11)   (12)

families who can get a good education.

Another way that schools are different from each other is in what they teach. Most

schools teach basic subjects, such as _____, _____, and
                                                (13)   (14)

_____. Other schools teach art, _____, and physical
        (15)   (16)

_____. But there are also special schools that _____ subjects
     (17)   (18)
such as auto mechanics, business skills, or dancing.

L O N G   R E A D I N G   1

PREREADING ACTIVITY

Almost everyone remembers something about his or her first day of school. It is
an important day in a child's life and in the life of the child's parents. Think about the
following questions and be prepared to answer them if your instructor asks you:

1. How old were you when you first went to school?
2. What was the name of the school you first went to?
3. Did one of your parents go to school with you on the first day?
4. How did you get to the school? How did you get home?
5. What was the name of your first teacher?
6. Do you remember anything special about the first day of school? Were you
excited? Were you happy? Did you cry?

Following are three descriptions of the first day of school, two from students and
one from a teacher. Read each description quickly, looking for the answers to these
two questions:

1. Was the student or the teacher happy about the first day of school?
2. What was one important memory the student or the teacher has from the first
day of school?

You should spend about five minutes reading each description and answering the
questions. The second question has more than one correct answer. Listen to what
other students have answered, and decide if their answers are also good ones.

The First Day of School

FIRST STUDENT

Although it has been many years since I first went to school, I can still   **1**
remember a lot about that day. When I tried to write about it, though, I found out
that I had forgotten a lot and had to talk with my mother to help remember just
what happened.

My parents had been talking about my going to school for weeks. They talked   **2**
about school in a way that made me think that I would have a good time there, so
when the first day came, I was not afraid. I woke up early, before my mother called

me. My mother had some new clothes for me and she made sure that I looked nice that day. I especially remember my new, red leather shoes. She made breakfast for me, and then we got in the car and drove to school. At the school we met the teacher, but we cannot remember her name. I do know that she was very nice to me and tried to make me feel comfortable in the classroom. The classroom was new, with brown plastic desks and a big green chalkboard at the front. There was an American flag, a set of pictures of the alphabet, and a clock on the wall. Along one wall was a set of boxes for storing our school supplies. The teacher had a big desk in a corner of the room. The room was, I think, light green.

I remember looking at all the new children who were in the class and wondering if I would like them or not. I also remember wondering whether the other students would laugh at my new school supplies. My mother had bought me a school bag with new pencils, crayons, and paper. I felt better, though, when I noticed that the other students had bags just like mine and were using the same pencils and crayons and paper. **3**

I was excited about school because I wanted to be able to write my name K-A-R-E-N, and my parents had promised me that after I had gone to school I would be able to do that. On that first day the teacher showed us all how to write our names. She also had written our names on the boxes along the wall and she showed us how to recognize our name and how to find our own box where we could keep our school supplies. **4**

I did meet a new friend that day, a girl named Miriam, who is still a friend of mine today. **5**

STOP READING *AND DO THE FOLLOWING:*

Answer the following questions.

1. Was this student happy about the first day of school?

_____

2. What was one important memory this student has from her first day of school?

_____

CONTINUE READING

SECOND STUDENT

My name is Mahmoud, and I went to school in my home country of Saudi Arabia. I am the youngest of five brothers, and I eagerly looked forward to the day when I could go to school with my brothers. I saw it as the day when I would stop being a child and begin being a man. **6**

The school year in Saudi Arabia begins in early September. The week before **7** school started, my father bought me a new school bag to carry my school supplies in. On the day that I first went to school he also gave me some money to buy snacks during the break between classes. On the first day I walked to school with my brothers. The school was only about twenty minutes from our home, so it was not too difficult to get there.

When I first walked into the classroom, I saw about thirty new faces that I had **8** never seen before. At that moment all of my eagerness about school began to disappear, and I began to cry from fear. My older brother, Abdul Rahim, was with me, and he tried to calm my fears by telling me that school would be fun and the other students would be my friends.

The schoolroom was full of large desks. At each desk four students were **9** already sitting. Each student had a drawer in the desk to keep his supplies in. The only other things I remember in the room, besides the teacher and his desk, were a chart of the Arabic alphabet and a map of our country.

First, the teacher asked us to write our names on a sheet of paper. Because **10** my family had prepared me well, I was able to write my own name, my father's name, and my family name. I was so good at writing that the teacher asked me to go to the blackboard and write the names there for everyone to see. Because I was so good at writing, I was put into the higher class. The students who could not write were put into a lower class. At that point I fell in love with school, and I have felt that way ever since.

STOP READING *AND DO THE FOLLOWING:*

Answer the following questions.

1. Was this student happy about the first day of school?

_____

2. What was one important memory this student has from his first day of school?

_____

CONTINUE READING

TEACHER

I have been teaching for seventeen years now. For the last three years I have **11** been teaching the second grade at Washington Elementary School. Most of what happens on the first day of school every year is not new for me because I have been doing it for too long. But I still approach each new school year differently.

One way that each year is different is that I always hope that each year's new **12** students will be different. I hope that this year's students will be smarter, better behaved, and more ready to settle down and start acting as though they are in school and not on vacation. I also hope that the new students will not cry, will have their lunch money, and will know what bus they are supposed to take to get home or whether their parents will be picking them up.

Another way I hope new school years will be different is that I hope I will be   **13** better prepared. I know that I have started school years before, so I should be ready to help the students organize their supplies and put them in the blue and red storage boxes at the back of the room. I should be ready for the children to get tired and start to fall asleep by two o'clock in the long afternoon. I should be ready to check that the students can write their names and can recognize their names when they see them.

But I am always surprised at the beginning of school. This year, for example,   **14** I had twenty-three new students. On the first day, six of them had forgotten to bring lunch money and did not have lunches of their own. I had to loan them money so they could eat in the cafeteria. Most of them knew how to get back home, but one little boy, Manfred, got on the wrong bus, and I had to pick him up and drive him home. He cried all the way.

I was also surprised this year when three of the students did not seem to be   **15** able to read, and one of them would not write her name. I had given them easy books to read after lunch, while I was trying to make up some lists of students' names for the office. I noticed that the three children were looking at the pictures in the book but not at the writing. I stopped and asked them what they were reading, but they did not seem to know. I hope that they were just confused and afraid on the first day of school and that they will be able to read along with the other children.

In general, though, the first day of school is an exciting one, for the children   **16** and for me. They are excited to get away from home and to be with a lot of other children their age. They look forward to the new year in school and ask me a lot of questions about what we will do during the year. I am excited because I have a new group of students to teach, and I look forward to watching them learn writing, mathematics, and information about the community and world they live in. Although it is sometimes difficult, it is very satisfying to be a teacher and to know that I am helping so many children become useful and educated adults.

STOP READING *AND DO THE FOLLOWING:*

Answer the following questions.

1. Was the teacher happy about the first day of school?

_____

2. What was one important memory the teacher has from her first day of school?

_____

INFORMATION EVALUATION

Now read the descriptions more carefully and fill in the following chart. Write *T* if the statement is true about that person, *F* if it is not, and *NI* if the information is not given in the reading.

	STUDENT 1	STUDENT 2	TEACHER
Had new clothes			
Had new supplies			
Found a new friend			
Was a little afraid on the first day			
Expected students to be smart			
Was in a class with thirty students			
Was able to write his/her name			
Walked to school			
Was excited about the first day			

COMPREHENSION QUESTIONS

Working with another student, answer the following questions without looking back at the descriptions. When you are finished, your instructor will ask you to compare your answers with those of other students in the class. Think about their answers and change any of your answers that you think are not correct.

1. How did the first student help to remember what happened on the first day of school?

_____

2. In what country did the first student go to school? Why do you think so?

_____

other U.S. citizens, he did not really learn to read or write in school and dropped out of school when he was fourteen years old. Michael was smart, and he was good at building things and at using machines. He was very successful as a construction worker and eventually started his own business. His wife helped him read and write what he needed, and he learned how to hide his inability from others. Finally, at the age of thirty-eight, Michael is going back to school to a special program to learn how to read and write. He is learning very quickly, partly because he is smart and partly because he knows how important reading and writing are to his work.

QUESTIONS

Look again at the questions from the beginning of the reading, and decide if you want to change any of your answers. Check with a partner to see if you agree on the answers. Write your answers on the lines following the questions.

1. Do you know any adults who cannot read and write? Are they trying to learn how to read and write? How are they trying? Do they think it is a problem that they cannot read and write?

_____

_____

_____

2. Do you know any adults who did not go to school for as long as they now think they should have? Are they going back to school or learning about their work in any other way?

_____

_____

_____

3. What kinds of subjects do adults need to study when they go to school?

_____

_____

_____

(Continued at top of next page)

4. Are adults better students than young people are? Why or why not?

_____

_____

_____

RESTATEMENT

The following sentences are taken from the reading. Rewrite the sentences in your own words to show that you understand their meaning. You may look back at the sentences in the reading to be sure you understand them. Work with a partner if your instructor asks you to.

Example:
Adult education programs are under way in Europe, in Asia, in Africa, and in South and North America.

Adult education programs have begun all over the world. _____

1. The basic belief behind adult education programs is that a country will be economically and politically stronger if its people are educated and are able to read, write, and do useful work.

_____

_____

_____

2. Adults have some advantages in education, however. Adult learners often know exactly what they need to learn.

_____

_____

_____

3. If they cannot read or write, they have experienced the problems that illiteracy can cause.

_____

_____

_____

4. If they cannot do their jobs well, they have experienced the loss of income or of job opportunities that lack of vocational training can cause.

_____

_____

_____

5. Adults have usually accumulated a wealth of experience of life in general that can help them in learning.

_____

_____

_____

COMPLETION

Read the following sentences. Then read the passage again and look for the information you need to complete the sentences. If your instructor asks you to, work with another student.

1. A country that has too many uneducated adults may have _____ and

_____ problems.

2. The three reasons why it may be difficult for adults to go back to school are

_____,

_____,

and _____.

3. One way to solve the problem of distance in adult education is _____

_____.

(Continued at top of next page)

4. Two advantages that adults have in education are _____

and _____ .

5. One reason that _____ is going back to school is _____

_____ .

6. Michael Johnson did not want his friends to know that _____

_____ .

INFORMATION CHECKING

Without looking back at the reading, mark the following sentences *T* for true, *F* for false, or *NI* if the information is not given in the reading. When you have finished, check your work by looking at the reading again.

1. _____ Governments want to educate adults so the adults will become rich.

2. _____ Adults are often afraid to go back to school, or they do not have enough time for school.

3. _____ Most villages in India have television sets.

4. _____ Adults are often more experienced, and their experience helps them become better learners.

5. _____ Chinese schools do not teach about electricity.

6. _____ Feng Lian is studying electricity so she can keep her job.

7. _____ Michael Johnson is now a carpenter.

8. _____ Michael Johnson goes to school at night.

VOCABULARY EXERCISE

1. In paragraph 2 there is a word that means "made a good guess." Write that

word here: _____

2. In paragraph 3 there is a word that means "something that stands in the way of," or "something that blocks or prevents movement."

Write that word here: _____

3. In paragraph 4 there is a phrase that means "been part of" or "helped to."

Write that phrase here: _____

4. In paragraph 4 there is a word that means the opposite of "city" or "urban."

Write that word here: _____

5. In paragraph 5 there is an adjective that means "work" or "occupational."

Write that word here: _____

Discuss your answers with other students until you all agree on the correct words.

PROBLEM SOLVING: GIVING ADVICE

James, a friend of yours, is in the tenth grade (the tenth year of school). James is not a very good student, mostly because he is not interested in school. He has an opportunity to get a full-time job, and his family needs money because his parents are both unable to work right now. James wants to drop out of school and go to work. He says that he does not need what they teach in school and that he can learn more and earn more if he stops going to school. James is not completely sure, though, and he has asked for your advice.

Discuss this with other students in a group. Working together, agree on some advice for James. Then compare your group's advice with the advice of other groups in class.

Write a letter to James giving him your advice. Your letter may be written by the whole class working together or by the students in your group. As you work together, be sure to agree on what you are going to include in your letter and to edit your letter to make it as correct as possible.

L O N G   R E A D I N G   3

PREREADING ACTIVITY

Read the following questions. Then scan the reading that follows them quickly (five or ten minutes), trying to find the answers.

1. What is the subject of this reading?
2. How many schools are described in the reading?
3. Where are the schools located?
4. What, in general, is the Japanese attitude toward education?

High Schools in Japan

The Japanese regard education very highly. Most Japanese have finished **1**
high school and the literacy rate in Japan is almost 100 percent. Sometimes
outsiders think that everything in Japan is standardized—that it is all the same.
That is somewhat true in education, but there are differences reflecting the
complexities of Japanese society and its long traditions. One way to observe
these differences is to examine five different high schools in Japan.

Otani is the name of one academic high school in Kobe. It is the most popular **2**
kind of high school in Japan today, because it is specifically designed to prepare
students to enter the university. The emphasis is on courses that prepare students
for the university entrance examination. Sixty-eight percent of all secondary
students are in schools with academic curriculums like Otani, and this includes
both public and private schools. The majority of students who attend Otani High
School come from families where the head of the family has a "white-collar" job.
There are few discipline problems; the students are very serious about going to
college to continue their education after they graduate from high school.

Nada, the most famous high school in Japan, is also in Kobe. It is a private **3**
boys' school in the eastern part of the city. Almost every year, Nada has
succeeded in placing more students in Tokyo University than any other school in
the country, even though the graduating classes are small. The average class
size is fifty-four. Nada is a very competitive and selective school. The boys
accepted into the school are in the top 1 percent of all who have taken an aptitude
test. Most of the students in this high school want to enter Japan's top universities.
Activities other than the academic ones are organized by the students. The
students are highly motivated.

Sakura, a boys' technical night school, is very different from the previously **4**
described schools. Most of the students at Sakura work in factories or at manual
jobs. Many of the students have problems in reading and, in general, they are not
very good students. The subjects taught at Sakura include courses that prepare
students for vocational fields, such as electronics. Most of the course work,
however, is aimed at preparing the students for college, since most of them want
to go on to further education. The teachers at Sakura High School are devoted to
the kind of vocational/academic teaching they do there and are very good at it.
Their job is a difficult one, but they try to teach the students as much as possible
under the conditions in which they have to work. There is a close and friendly
atmosphere among the students and faculty at Sakura.

A fourth high school in Kobe is Okada High School. Okada is a school **5**
especially devoted to maintaining Japanese social traditions. In addition to the

regular college preparation curriculum, the courses and teaching methods at Okada follow the old Japanese traditions of respect and politeness toward elders and a knowledge of the history and older literature of the country. There is a great deal of ritual and ceremony in the way teachers and students behave toward each other. There are few disciplinary problems and most of Okada's students go on to college.

Yama is the fifth high school in Kobe. It is a vocational high school for both **6** boys and girls. The students in Yama are not very motivated, and not as intelligent as the students in some other schools. The students in Yama High School are not planning on going on to college. The curriculum is completely oriented toward training the students for work immediately after high school. Yama has a greater problem with discipline than any of the other schools.

There is quite a bit of variety among the high schools in Japan. The five **7** schools described above are examples of the major types of schools found in Japan. Each of the five is different in the type of instruction, the goals of the students, and the seriousness of discipline problems. There are also similarities. They are all part of the strong Japanese educational tradition, they take their responsibility seriously, and they are operated on the same tradition of politeness and respect found in most Japanese social institutions.

QUESTIONS

Now write your answers to the questions from the beginning of the reading. Then work together with another student to correct your answers.

1. What is the subject of this reading? (Answer this in one sentence.)

_____

_____

2. How many schools are described in the reading?

_____

3. Where are the schools located?

_____

4. What, in general, is the Japanese attitude toward education?

_____

Read the passage again more slowly (ten to fifteen minutes), and then do the following exercises.

SUMMARY WRITING

Using the following questions as a guide, write a summary of the reading.

1. Are all Japanese high schools basically the same?
2. What is important about Otani High School?
3. What is important about Nada High School?
4. What is important about Sakura High School?
5. What is important about Okada High School?
6. What is important about Yama High School?
7. What is the writer's conclusion about high schools in Japan?

Compare your summary with summaries written by other students. Did you all include the same information? Who wrote the longest summary? Do you think it is too long? Who wrote the shortest summary? Do you think it is too short?

INFORMATION CHECKING

The numbered sentences on the next page give information about high schools in Japan. Write the number of the sentence after the name of the high school about

which it is true. Each sentence may be true about more than one school. The first one has been done for you.

Otani: _____   Nada: _____

Sakura: __1_____   Okada: _____

Yama: _____

1. The school has classes at night.
2. All students in the school are male.
3. There are few discipline problems in the school.
4. The students in this school organize activities.
5. The school is concerned with preserving Japanese tradition.
6. The students from this school usually do not go to college.
7. In this school the students learn work skills.
8. The parents of the students in the school are generally white-collar workers.
9. Politeness is emphasized in the school.
10. Students must take a test to enter the school.
11. The school is in the eastern part of Kobe.
12. The students in this school often have reading problems.
13. This is a vocational school.
14. This is an academic preparatory school.
15. The students in the school also have jobs.
16. Most college students went to a school like this.

INFORMATION SELECTION

Each of the five schools described in the reading is special or unique in some way. Under the name of each school given below and on the next page, list one or more facts that are true only of that school.

Otani: Okada:

_____   _____

_____   _____

_____   _____

Nada: Yama:

_____   _____

_____   _____

_____   _____

Sakura:

_____

_____

_____

VOCABULARY EXERCISE

On the left is a list of words from the reading. The number after the word tells which paragraph the word is in. On the right is a list of definitions. There are more definitions than there are words to define. Write the number of each word in the space before its definition.

1. regard (1)   _____ feeling that exists in a place

2. complexities (1)   _____ acting or behaving in a good way

3. traditions (1)   _____ take a test

4. examine (1)   _____ finishing or completing school

5. emphasis (2)   _____ best

6. discipline (2)   _____ keeping

7. graduating (3)   _____ many different parts

8. top (3)   _____ look at carefully

9. atmosphere (4)   _____ think about

10. maintaining (5)   _____ related differences

                          _____ customs from the past

                          _____ strong attention

WRITING: INTERVIEW

Interview another student about two different high schools or universities in his or her home country. Write the description as a short paragraph. Give the completed paragraph to the student you interviewed for checking. Your instructor may ask you to read your paragraph to the whole class.

CROSSWORD PUZZLE

Fill in the crossword puzzle on page 29 with words related to education.

ACROSS

5. The first years of school.
7. Biology, zoology, and physics are all kinds of _____.
8. We hate this and have to do it after school.
9. Students go to school to _____.
10. Some students go to a _____ after high school.
12. The science of numbers.
14. Some people write with a _____.
17. The teacher usually writes on this at the front of the room.
19. To begin to write we need to know the _____.
20. A _____ tells us how much we have learned.
21. When you don't do well on an exam, you _____.
22. Very similar to a test.

DOWN

1. What we get after we take a test.
2. Someone who has the ability to learn easily is called _____.
3. This is where teachers work.
4. My favorite _____ is history.
6. Right now I am taking an English _____.
11. The second level of education.
13. We learn because teachers _____.
15. It helps to study with a _____.
16. When you do well on a exam, you _____.
18. Some people write with a _____.

CHAPTER REVIEW

In this chapter you have read about the back-to-basics movement in education in the United States. You have also read about the first day of school for several people, adult education throughout the world, and high schools in Kobe, Japan. Answer the following questions about the readings. Work alone and answer for yourself. Most of the questions do not have one correct answer; the answers are your opinion or are true for you. When you are finished, discuss your answers with your instructor and the rest of the class.

1. Which reading did you learn the most from? Why?

_____

_____

_____

2. Write five pieces of information that you learned from reading this chapter.

a. _____

_____

b. _____

_____

c. _____

_____

d. _____

_____

e. _____

_____

3. Which reading was the most interesting? Why?

_____

_____

_____

4. Which reading was the easiest to read? Why?

_____

_____

5. Which reading was the most difficult to read? Why?

_____

_____

6. Which reading had the most personal experience or opinion in it?

_____

7. Which reading had the most research in it?

_____

Now that you have read and thought about education, write three questions that you have about education.

Example:
Do students in the Soviet Union have to pay to go to a college or university?

1. _____

2. _____

3. _____

Working in groups or as a class, agree on three questions that you think are the most interesting. Then, as a group, decide where you might find the answers to these questions. You might need to look in a particular book or encyclopedia, or interview a particular person. If there is time, go as a group and find the answers to the questions.

WRITING OR SPEAKING SUMMARY

Choose one of the following topics. Then using the information and language you have learned in this chapter, write at least one page on that topic or prepare to talk to the class about it.

1. Describe the best teacher you ever had. Why was he or she good? What did you learn from that teacher?

2. What are three changes you want to make in the educational system in your home country or in the country where you are studying? Give reasons for your changes.

3. Describe the two best experiences you have had in school and the two worst experiences. Explain why they were good and why they were bad.

READING JOURNAL

List the outside reading you did while studying this chapter. (Include the title or type of material, length, topic or subject, and where you found the material.)

_____

_____

_____

Write a journal entry for this outside reading. Your instructor will want to look at your journal and may ask you to tell the class about something you read. In your journal you might answer the following questions. Or you can write about anything else you felt or learned as you were reading.

What was the most interesting thing you read? Why was it interesting?

What was the least interesting thing you read? Why was it not interesting?

What is one piece of information you learned about education from your outside reading?

Was the reading you did difficult or easy? Why do you think it was difficult or easy?

Do you have questions about education that you can find the answers to by reading? What are they? What can you read to find the answers?

Did you enjoy the outside reading you did while you studied this chapter? Why or why not?

Chapter
2
GETTING
THE NEWS

All the news that's fit to print.
—Adolph S. Ochs

INTRODUCTION

The phrase at the top of this page is printed on the front page of every edition of the *New York Times*. Working in pairs or in groups, write several sentences explaining what this phrase means. You may ask your instructor or someone else who speaks English well to help you.

When you have finished, read your group's explanation to the rest of the class. As a class, determine which group has the best explanation. Then, in groups again, decide if this is a good rule for a newspaper to follow. Again, each group should share its opinion with the rest of the class.

VOCABULARY INTRODUCTION

In this chapter you will be reading about the subject of news and information. Before you read, look at the words below and work with a group of other students in the class to see if you know what these words mean. If you do not know, ask other students, ask your instructor, or look in a dictionary to find out what they mean. Write the definition of each word you did not know on the blank lines at the top of the next page.

broadcast	headline	radio
communicate	information	report
copy	news	reporter
daily	newspaper	story
document	paper	telephone
edition	print	write
editor	publish	writer

DEFINITIONS OF WORDS YOU DID NOT KNOW:

1. _____

2. _____

3. _____

4. _____

5. _____

6. _____

7. _____

8. _____

On the lines below, write ten other words that you think are related to news and information. When you are finished, you or your instructor can write the words that the class thought of on the blackboard.

_____	_____	_____
_____	_____	_____
_____	_____	_____
_____		

Write on the lines below any word written on the blackboard that you are not sure you know the meaning of.

_____	_____	_____
_____	_____	_____
_____	_____	_____

Review these words as you complete this chapter.

OUTSIDE READING

Doing outside reading about news and communication will help you to understand this chapter better. Magazines and newspapers are good examples of how different countries present the news. Embassies and consulates usually provide news bulletins. Almanacs give statistics about newspapers and radio and television stations. Television schedules contain information about what programs are broadcast.

Take a few minutes in class and suggest outside readings about news and information and where to find them. Write on the lines below some good suggestions that you hear.

_____

_____

_____

_____

_____

Be sure to write about your outside reading in your Reading Journal.

INFORMATION GATHERING

Working in four groups, find out about the available sources of news and information in your community or area. Have each group work on one of the following categories. List the names of as many sources as you can, as well as any other important information. Bring the lists to class, and see if the other students can add to the lists.

Group 1: Radio Stations

What are the names ("call letters") of the stations? How often does each station broadcast news? Is the news local, national, or both? What else do the stations broadcast? Are there both AM and FM stations? How many of each?

Group 2: Television Stations

Is television available? If it is, are programs available through broadcasting or by cable? How many channels are available? What are the names ("call letters") of the most important stations? What channel numbers do they have? How often does each station broadcast news? At what times? Is the news local, national, or both? Is the station a member of a network? Which one? What else do the stations broadcast?

Group 3: Newspapers

What newspapers are easy to find and buy in the community? How many are there? Are they published locally, in a nearby city, or nationally? Is the emphasis of the news in each paper local or national? Do any of the newspapers have a special interest (financial news, sports, entertainment, etc.)? How often is each

paper published? How much does it cost? Does it have any special interest for
students in the class?

Group 4: Newsmagazines
What newsmagazines are available? Are they local or national? What kinds of news
do they publish? How often is each magazine published? How much does it cost?
Where can it be bought? Are there any magazines that are especially interesting to
students in the class?

Use the information your group collected to write a directory for the other
students in the class or in the school. Indicate why the news sources are, or should be,
interesting to the readers of the directory.

S H O R T   R E A D I N G

PREREADING ACTIVITY

Read the following questions. See if you know the answers to any of them. Then
read the passage about the development of television to find the answers to the
questions. Read carefully, taking about ten minutes.

1. What invention was necessary before television could be developed?
2. What could Vladimir Zworykin's invention do?
3. What event occurred between the time Zworykin invented the television camera
and the time television became popular?
4. Why were early televisions limited to black and white?
5. What is the relationship between satellites and television broadcasts?

The Development of Television

Television was not really invented. Many scientists invented or improved parts   1
of the system that have become the television systems we know now. Radio, of
course, was necessary before television could be developed, because television
uses the same principles of electromagnetic waves that radio does. As soon as
radio became possible in the 1800s, the possibility of television transmission was
also known, but it took many years for it to become practical.

British and American scientists helped to develop the basic ideas that made   2
television possible, but it was a Russian who made the first practical television
system. By 1923, Vladimir Zworykin, a Russian, had invented a camera tube that
could turn pictures into electric energy. By 1929, Zworykin had built a television
system that worked.

By 1935, regular television broadcasts were begun in Germany. The first   3
broadcasts in the United States began in 1939, but television did not really

become popular until after the Second World War. Between 1945 and 1955 there was rapid growth in the practical use of television.

All early television was broadcast in black and white. Color television was possible, but it was too expensive and of very poor quality until the middle of the 1950s. Color television broadcasts began in the United States in 1954, in Japan in 1960, and in Europe in 1967. **4**

The first landing on the moon was broadcast live on television in 1969, and now television programs are sent all over the world immediately through the use of satellites that transmit the signals from the earth, through space, and back to earth. **5**

More people now get their news and information through television than through newspapers and radio. The development of television is one of the most rapid and exciting events of our century. **6**

QUESTIONS

Now write your answers to the questions from the beginning of the reading.

1. What invention was necessary before television could be developed?

_____

_____

2. What could Vladimir Zworykin's invention do?

_____

_____

3. What event occurred between the time Zworykin invented the television camera and the time television became popular?

_____

_____

4. Why were early televisions limited to black and white?

_____

_____

(Continued at top of next page)

5. What is the relationship between satellites and television broadcasts?

_____

_____

FILL-IN-THE-BLANK

Working with another student, fill in the blanks in the following passage. For many of the blanks, more than one answer will be possible or correct, but put only one word in each blank. Look carefully at the sentences that come before and after the blank to be sure that the word you choose has meaning in both the sentence and the paragraph and that the form of the word is correct for that sentence. Discuss with your partner any differences in the words you choose, your understanding of the sentences, and your reasons for choosing certain words. The purpose of the exercise is to try to find as many words that can fit in the blanks as possible.

When you and your partner have finished, your instructor will ask you to compare your answers with the answers that your classmates gave. Your instructor may ask you to write your words on the blackboard. Be ready to explain why you chose a word and what the word means. Also be ready to change your answer if other students found a better word. Write other good answers that you hear below the ones that you gave.

Where Do We Get the News?

Information about what has happened in the world, in our country, in our area,

or even in our town comes to us in many ways. People who can read often get the

_____ from _____. Since many people in the world are
      (1)   (2)

illiterate, however, they have to get their news from _____ or
                                                            (3)

_____ .
      (4)

Newspapers around the world are similar in many ways. They all

_____ news stories that tell readers about the events of the day or week.
      (5)

Most newspapers include editorials that give the _____ of the government
                                                      (6)

or of the newspaper's publishers.

Often, papers have other _____ that are devoted to business, sports,
                              (7)

and maybe the latest fashion news. Papers usually appear _____, or every
(8)

day, but in some places they may only appear _____.
(9)

_____ are another way that some people get the news. Magazines are
(10)

longer and usually appear _____. _____ and _____
(11)   (12)   (13)

are two other sources of news. They get the news out faster than newspapers and

magazines, and they do not have to be read. Radio and television stations

_____ the news several times every day.
(14)

L O N G   R E A D I N G   1

PREREADING ACTIVITY

Read the following questions carefully. When you are sure you understand the
questions, scan the reading that follows to find the answers.

1. What is the subject or topic of the reading?
2. Why is the subject important?
3. When was the invention described in the reading invented?
4. What is one important use of the invention?

Carlson's Invention

When we think of inventions or developments that have improved the communication of information, most of us think of things such as the telephone, the radio, the telegraph, and the television. But there is one invention that has affected communication almost as much as those inventions that communicate voices and pictures. It is an invention that improved the communication of written or printed information. Can you guess what that invention is?   **1**

First, a clue to help you. Printing, or making copies of writing by machine, was invented in the 1400s, both in Korea and in Europe. Before that time, if people wanted copies of a written document, they had to write it out by themselves or pay another writer to make the copy. Making copies was, therefore, very slow and very expensive, and it was always possible that the copy would not be a perfect one. It might have mistakes that made it different from the original.   **2**

After printing was invented, it became possible to make many copies of a written document, and every copy was the same. Written and printed information   **3** became very easily available. But the process of printing a document is always complex and often expensive. It was too complex and too expensive to be used to make quick copies of short documents such as letters or pages of books.

In 1938, a man named Chester Carlson invented a machine that could make **4** single copies of written documents cheaply and quickly. Since that time, his invention has spread throughout the world and has almost replaced printing in some places as a way of making copies of a single written document. Have you guessed what that invention is?

You may have guessed the invention, but you may not know exactly what its **5** name is. The invention was xerography, or the making of copies by a dry, mechanical process. The process is more commonly known now as photocopying, although it does not involve making a photograph.

Most of us have used a photocopy machine, but few of us really know how **6** it works. The details are very complex, but the basic process is simple. First, the original document that we want a copy of, a page of printing or a picture, is illuminated by a bright light. The pattern of light and dark in the document is reflected onto a smooth metal drum or cylinder. A powder sticks to the drum in the places where there was darkness in the original picture. A piece of plain paper is then passed near the drum. Electricity on the back of the paper causes the powder to move from the drum to the paper. Heat on the paper then causes the powder to stick to the paper permanently, making a permanent copy of the original document.

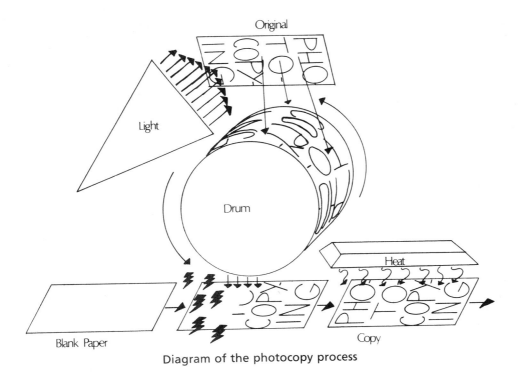

Diagram of the photocopy process

Chester Carlson developed the xerography or photocopy process in 1937, **7** but the first photocopy machines were not sold until the early 1960s. In thirty years, however, photocopying has become common throughout the world. It is widely used in business to make copies of important documents such as letters and contracts without typing or writing them out many times, as was done earlier. Photocopying has replaced printing for many documents that are needed quickly and that do not have to be of high quality. Advertising, restaurant menus, announcements of meetings, and legal documents such as birth and death records and records of changes in residence or employment are often copied. Many people also use photocopies just to make a copy of a picture, a story, or a recipe they thought was interesting so they can keep it for themselves or send it to friends.

Photocopying is also used in education to make copies of lessons and tests **8** prepared by the teacher. Students often make copies of books that are difficult to buy, and this has created problems when the book is copyrighted. That is, when an author or company owns the material in the book and has not given permission to anyone else to print or make copies of that material. The problem is especially serious if the person making the copies can benefit financially from making the copies. Making copies of copyrighted books is illegal in most countries, and the companies that own the copyright have tried hard to see that photocopies of their material are not made.

Certainly, the photocopy machine is not as common as the telephone or **9** radio, but it has affected the way that information is spread and the amount of information that is available almost as much. New developments related to photocopying, such as telephone facsimile or fax machines and high-quality computer printers, are also helping to make the communication of written material more efficient.

QUESTIONS

Now write your answers to the questions from the beginning of the reading.

1. What is the subject or topic of the reading?

_____

2. Why is the subject important?

_____

3. When was the invention described in the reading invented?

_____

(Continued at top of next page)

4. What is one important use of the invention?

_____

Compare your answers with those of your classmates. Did you all give the same answers? If not, is more than one answer correct? Why did you give different answers?

Now read the passage again more slowly (about twenty minutes). Then do the following exercises.

COMPLETION

Working with a partner, complete the following sentences with information from the reading. When you are finished, your instructor will ask you to compare your answers with those of the other students in the class. Be prepared to show where in the reading you found your answers.

Printing was invented in the 1400s in _____ and in _____.

Printing is too _____ and _____ to be used for quick copies

of short documents. Carlson's invention, the _____ machine, is

_____ and _____ than printing. To photocopy a document, you

must first _____ the document with a bright light. A copy of the document

is made on a _____ drum. The picture on the drum is transferred to a piece

of _____ and is made permanent by _____.

People using a photocopy machine must be very careful not to copy

any _____ material. _____, _____, and

_____ are some of the kinds of documents that are commonly photocop-

ied. _____ or fax machines send copies of documents over tele-

phone lines.

SUMMARY WRITING

Using the following questions as a guide, write a short summary of the reading.

1. What problem with copies of documents existed before the photocopy machine was developed?

2. Who invented the photocopy machine and when?
3. How does the photocopy machine work? (Answer in one or two sentences.)
4. What is most frequently copied on photocopy machines?

Compare your summary with summaries written by other students. Did you all include the same information? Who wrote the longest summary? Do you think it is too long? Who wrote the shortest summary? Do you think it is too short?

VOCABULARY EXERCISE

Circle the best answer.

1. In paragraph 1 you read the word *affected*. The best meaning for *affected* in that paragraph is:

a. made better

b. modernized

c. hurt or damaged

d. changed

2. In paragraph 2 you read the word *clue*. The best meaning for *clue* in that paragraph is:

a. a lie, an untruth

b. a piece of information that helps solve a problem

c. a joke

d. something that is written

3. In paragraph 2 you read the word *document*. The best meaning for *document* in that paragraph is:

a. something that is printed or written

b. a picture

c. a copy

d. a person who writes

4. In paragraph 4 you read the word *spread*. The best meaning for *spread* in that paragraph is:

a. been sold

b. become more widely known and used

c. become more expensive and complex

d. been invented

5. In paragraph 6 you read the word *details*. The best meaning for *details* in that paragraph is:

a. important parts

b. price or cost

c. buttons or knobs that control

d. small pieces or parts

CONTEST

Your instructor will give each of you a document to copy by hand and will time you to see how long it takes. The winner will be the one who copies the document in the shortest time and with the fewest mistakes. Each mistake will add 10 percent to the time it took to copy the document.

Add up the time it took for each student in class to make the copy. Compare that to the time it would take to make a photocopy of the document for each student in the class:

hand copy _____   photocopy _____
                (total time)   (total time)

L O N G   R E A D I N G   2

PREREADING ACTIVITY

Many people believe everything or almost everything they read in newspapers or hear on the radio. They think that if information has been printed or broadcast, someone must have checked to see that it was true. The following reading describes some stories that may not be true.

Before you read, look at the following questions and scan the reading to find the answers.

1. Where did the couple leave the baby in the first story?
2. What finally happened to the baby?
3. Why do people believe stories like the one about the baby?
4. What kind of fear does the second story represent?
5. Why does the woman crash her Mercedes into the other car in the third story?
6. Do you think the story about the woman in the Mercedes is funny? Why or why not?

But I Read It in the Paper!

A few years ago I read a story about a husband and wife who made a terrible   1
mistake. They had gone shopping and had taken their small baby along with them. After they had finished their shopping, they returned to their car to go home. When they reached their car, they put the baby in the plastic baby carrier that he rode in for safety. The couple then drove off in their car toward home. After they had driven a few miles, they looked in the back seat of the car to see how the baby was. To their surprise, the baby was not there. According to the story, the couple had put the plastic seat and the baby on the top of the car but had forgotten to put him inside the car. They had driven away with the baby on the top of the car.

The couple drove back toward the store but did not find the baby. They called   2
the police, and the police said that they had the baby and that the baby was fine. The baby had fallen from the top of the car but had been protected by his plastic seat. The grateful couple took their baby home and were always careful after that.

There was one thing wrong with the story. It was not true. Even though it had **3** been published in a major newspaper, the story was a myth or rumor, a story that many people believe but is simply not true. I believed the story because I had read it in a newspaper. I made the mistake of thinking that information reported in newspapers is usually true. Often it is, but there are stories that get into the news that are not true but that sound as though they could be true. Newspaper and radio reporters like to repeat them because they are interesting.

Stories such as this one are often reported in newspapers and on radio and **4** television. Because they are read and heard in places that usually report the truth, many people believe them. People also believe them because, like the story above, they have something unusual or frightening about them. What is strange is that newspaper and radio reporters also believe them.

Another untrue story that has been reported in many places is a story that **5** shows how some people are afraid and suspicious of strangers. The story has many variations, but in most of them some group of Chinese or Southeast Asian people living in the United States is described as eating dogs and other pets as food. The story is based on the partly true belief many Americans have that many Chinese regularly eat the meat of dogs. Because Americans think this is a strange and unacceptable custom, they show their fear of strangers by spreading false stories such as this one. Newspapers and radio only help to spread this kind of untruth and rumor.

A funnier rumor that has appeared in many papers in the world is a story **6** about an older, rich woman who is trying to find a place to park her Mercedes Benz. A parking place opens up and just as she is about to drive into it, a younger driver with an old car drives into the parking place first. The younger driver says, "I'm young and fast." The older woman calmly crashes her Mercedes into the old car several times and says to the surprised driver, "But I'm old and rich."

The story is funny to some readers. Others think it is just silly. But the story has **7** appeared in many newspapers in the world and has been reported as true. But it never happened. It is another example of the stories that spread and are published because some people want to believe them, even if they are not true.

QUESTIONS

Now write your answers to the questions from the beginning of the reading.

1. Where did the couple leave the baby in the first story?

_____

2. What finally happened to the baby?

_____

(Continued at top of next page)

3. Why do people believe stories like the one about the baby?

_____

4. What kind of fear does the second story represent?

_____

5. Why does the woman crash her Mercedes into the other car in the third story?

_____

6. Do you think the story about the woman in the Mercedes is funny? Why or why not?

_____

_____

_____

Compare your answers with those of other students in the class. Did you all write the same information? If not, what was different and why?

COMPREHENSION QUESTIONS

Read the passage again more slowly and thoroughly. It should take about fifteen or twenty minutes. Then work with a partner to answer the following questions:

1. Why do you think people believe that the baby in the first story was not hurt?

_____

2. In the story, how do you think the police could have got the baby?

_____

3. How do you think the newspaper could have got the story about the baby?

_____

4. Why do we repeat stories about the strange things that people from different countries or cultures do?

_____

5. Why would newspapers print stories that are not true?

_____

VOCABULARY EXERCISE

Below are five phrases that appear in the reading. Working with a partner, write definitions for each word in the phrase and then for the two words together. Compare your answers with those of other students, and write the best definitions that you hear.

Example:
suspicious stranger

suspicious: *something that seems to be bad or not right*

stranger: *someone who is not known or familiar*

suspicious stranger: *an unfamiliar or unknown person who may be bad or*

dangerous

terrible mistake (paragraph 1)

terrible: _____

mistake: _____

terrible mistake: _____

_____

grateful couple (paragraph 2)

grateful: _____

couple: _____

grateful couple: _____

_____

radio reporters (paragraph 3)

radio: _____

reporters: _____

radio reporters: _____

_____

unacceptable custom (paragraph 5)

unacceptable: _____

custom: _____

unacceptable custom: _____

_____

parking place (paragraph 6)

parking: _____

place: _____

parking place: _____

_____

INFORMATION EVALUATION

Rumors are often spread about famous people. In the 1960s, for example, a rumor began about the musical group the Beatles. The rumor was that one member of the group, Paul McCartney, was dead, and that the Beatles were trying to hide him by substituting another man who looked just like him. Many newspapers and radio stations repeated this rumor, and it stayed around for a long time.

Many countries have magazines or newspapers that specialize in printing stories about famous people that may or may not be true. Often the stories are just rumors. If you can, bring to class a newspaper or magazine of this kind, and tell the other students what stories you think are rumors and why.

L O N G   R E A D I N G   3

PREREADING ACTIVITY

The following reading is about newspapers. It describes what makes a good newspaper and describes three newspapers from around the world that seem to be good newspapers.

The reading is divided into four parts, with exercises after each part. Look over all four parts quickly (in about ten minutes), and answer the following questions:

1. What does the word *circulation* mean?

_____

2. How many characteristics of good newspapers are given?

_____

3. Who identified these characteristics?

_____

4. How many newspapers are described?

_____

5. What countries are the newspapers from?

_____

Now read more carefully, taking about twenty minutes, and do the exercises after each part.

Read All About It!

Although only about half of the people in the world are literate, newspapers **1** play an important role in bringing news and information to those who can read or who hear about the news from people who can read. Almost every country in the world has newspapers, and most have many, many different papers. Even a small country like Nepal, north of India, has more than ten different newspapers in three different languages.

Not everyone reads newspapers, however. *Circulation* is the word that is used **2** to indicate how many newspapers are actually printed in a country. If a country has one million people and every day one million newspapers are printed and sold, then the circulation of newspapers in that country is one newspaper for every one person. No country prints that many newspapers. The country with the highest circulation of newspapers is the Soviet Union, where there are about 770 newspapers printed and sold for every 1,000 people. Japan also has a high circulation rate. There, about 50 newspapers are sold for every 100 people; about 50 percent of the population buys a newspaper. The rate of literacy, or the percentage of people who can read and write, is almost 100 percent in these two countries.

In the United States and in many countries in Europe, literacy is also high **3**
but newspaper circulation is much lower, at about 25 for every 100 people
(25 percent). Not surprisingly, in less developed countries where literacy is below 50 percent, newspaper circulation is sometimes as low as 2 for every 100
people.

What Is a Good Newspaper?

In their book, *The World's Great Dailies,* John Merrill and Harold Fisher (1980) **4**
give us the opinions of many professional newspaper writers about what
makes a newspaper great. The writers generally agreed on the following characteristics:

1. The paper should be independent and free from governmental or political
control.
2. The paper should include a broad range of topics, including social,
political, economic, scientific, and cultural topics.
3. The paper should have an international interest and should include news
and information from many parts of the world.
4. The paper should have a clear opinion on the news it reports.
5. The paper should attempt to improve knowledge and to influence opinion.

STOP READING *AND DO THE FOLLOWING:*

Listed below are the five characteristics of a great newspaper given in the reading. After each are two sentences, one of which means basically the same thing as
the sentence in the reading. Put a check (√) before the sentence with the same
meaning as the sentence in the reading. Work with a partner if your instructor asks
you to.

1. The paper should be independent and free from governmental or political
control.

_____ a. The government should control the newspaper carefully.

_____ b. Government and politics should not control the newspaper.

2. The paper should include a broad range of topics, including social, political,
economic, scientific, and cultural topics.

_____ a. The newspaper should contain articles about many different subjects.

_____ b. The newspaper should be about science and politics.

3. The paper should have an international interest and should include news and information from many parts of the world.

_____ a. The newspaper should not be of international interest.

_____ b. News and information should not be only from the city or country where the newspaper is published.

4. The paper should have a clear opinion on the news it reports.

_____ a. The newspaper should include news but not opinions.

_____ b. Clearly written opinions are important in a good newspaper.

5. The paper should attempt to improve knowledge and to influence opinion.

_____ a. The newspaper should include articles that try to educate the public.

_____ b. The newspaper should be influenced by public opinion.

When you have completed the exercise, discuss your answers with other students in the class. When all of the students agree on the answers, continue reading.

CONTINUE READING

In their book, Merrill and Fisher describe fifty newspapers that have the **5** characteristics listed above. The authors say there are many great newspapers in the world but that they had to limit their descriptions to the fifty best ones. The papers they describe are from all parts of the world, North and South America, Asia, and Europe. Three papers they selected are _Al Ahram_ from Egypt, the _Straits Times_ from Singapore, and the _Christian Science Monitor_ from the United States.

Al Ahram is written in Arabic. It is not the biggest newspaper in Egypt **6** because another newspaper, _Al Akhbar,_ has a higher circulation. _Al Ahram_ is a daily newspaper and is read all over the country of Egypt. About one million copies of it are printed every day. Some of these copies of the newspaper are sent to other Arabic-speaking countries in the Middle East, and the newspaper is also widely read in North and South America and in Europe. It is, therefore, also a very international newspaper.

Al Ahram usually has about eighteen pages. The first pages contain important **7** national and international news. Other pages and sections of the paper are about political opinions, local news, and sports. Also included are letters to the editor, a women's page, and notices of people's deaths. About one half of the paper is made up of advertising, sometimes in color. Many of Egypt's best writers write or have written for _Al Ahram_. The quality of its writing and of its news and political opinion is respected throughout the Arabic-speaking world.

STOP READING *AND DO THE FOLLOWING:*

Look again at the five characteristics of great newspapers. Which of these characteristics are true about *Al Ahram?*

1. The paper should be independent and free from governmental or political control.

True _____   Not true _____   Cannot answer from the reading _____

2. The paper should include a broad range of topics, including social, political, economic, scientific, and cultural topics.

True _____   Not true _____   Cannot answer from the reading _____

3. The paper should have an international interest and should include news and information from many parts of the world.

True _____   Not true _____   Cannot answer from the reading _____

4. The paper should have a clear opinion on the news it reports.

True _____   Not true _____   Cannot answer from the reading _____

5. The paper should attempt to improve knowledge and to influence opinion.

True _____   Not true _____   Cannot answer from the reading _____

Discuss your answers with the rest of the class. When all the students agree on the answers, continue reading.

CONTINUE READING

The *Straits Times* is an English-language newspaper from the small country of Singapore in Southeast Asia. Although the population of Singapore is just over two million, and English is only one of four official languages, the *Straits Times* is one of the most respected newspapers in Southeast Asia. It became so popular in nearby Malaysia that, beginning in 1956, the paper began to print a separate Malaysian edition. Although widely read, the circulation of the *Straits Times* is much smaller than that of *Al Ahram*. Its total circulation is around 200,000 copies every day.   **8**

The *Straits Times* has a clear, simple appearance. The first of its thirty pages contains important international news stories with short but factual headlines. In fact, about 20 percent of the news in the paper is international news. Also on the first page are important regional news stories and some advertising. Advertising makes up about one half of the total space in the paper.   **9**

The *Straits Times* is not a conservative paper, but it does not take any extreme   **10**
political positions. It attempts to inform and explain rather than to convince its
readers of an opinion or point of view. The *Straits Times* is a small, English-
language newspaper that is widely read and respected in a well-populated part
of the world where English serves as an important means of communication.

STOP READING *AND DO THE FOLLOWING:*

Which of the characteristics of great newspapers are true about the *Straits
Times?*

1. The paper should be independent and free from governmental and political
control.

True _____   Not true _____   Cannot answer from the reading _____

2. The paper should include a broad range of topics, including social, political,
economic, scientific, and cultural topics.

True _____   Not true _____   Cannot answer from the reading _____

3. The paper should have an international interest and should include news and
information from many parts of the world.

True _____   Not true _____   Cannot answer from the reading _____

4. The paper should have a clear opinion on the news it reports.

True _____   Not true _____   Cannot answer from the reading _____

5. The paper should attempt to improve knowledge and to influence opinion.

True _____   Not true _____   Cannot answer from the reading _____

Discuss your answers with the rest of the class. When all the students agree on
the answers, continue reading.

CONTINUE READING

Many visitors to the United States complain that newspapers there do not do   **11**
a very good job at reporting international news. They are partly correct because
most newspapers in the United States are local or regional papers. That is, they
are published in one city or area and contain news and advertising that is of
interest primarily to that city or area. One exception to the local interest of most
U.S. papers is the *Christian Science Monitor*.

The *Christian Science Monitor* is one of only two or three national newspapers   **12**
in the United States. The paper is also unusual because it is one of the few
important papers in the United States or the world that is owned by a church, the
First Church of Christ, Scientist. The purpose of the newspaper is not to spread
the religious beliefs of the church, however, and the paper cannot be called a
church newspaper. The purposes of the *Christian Science Monitor* are the same
as those of any good newspaper, to inform readers of news they need to know
and to do this in an independent and convincing way.

The *Christian Science Monitor* fulfills its purpose well. More than 200,000   **13**
people all over the United States read its twenty-five- to thirty-page daily editions,
and these are some of the best educated and important people in the country.
The president and members of Congress read the *Christian Science Monitor,* and
copies are sent to almost every embassy in Washington, D.C. The newspaper is
also read regularly by government leaders in all parts of the world and by the
editors of other newspapers.

The success of the *Christian Science Monitor* is due, in part, to its excellent   **14**
reporting of international news stories. It collects much of this information itself
using more than fifty reporters all over the world. It also prints important news from
the United States, often in long reports that provide the background of a story as
well as the most recent news. These background articles are an important part of
the newspaper, and at least once a week the paper includes a section of several
pages that explains and reports on a single story by giving the history and
significance of that story. The reporting in the paper is honest, complete, and
balanced. All points of view are represented, but the paper's editors do state
editorial opinion. The writing is clear and of high quality.

In addition to its extensive national and international news coverage, the   **15**
Christian Science Monitor contains many special sections on books, education,
finance, food, sports, travel, science, and arts and entertainment. The only way in
which the interests of the church that owns the paper are represented is through
a daily religious essay.

STOP READING   *AND DO THE FOLLOWING:*

Which of the characteristics of great newspapers are true about the *Christian Science Monitor?*

1. The paper should be independent and free from government or political control.

True _____   Not true _____   Cannot answer from the reading _____

2. The paper should include a broad range of topics, including social, political, economic, scientific, and cultural topics.

True _____   Not true _____   Cannot answer from the reading _____

3. The paper should have an international interest and should include news and information from many parts of the world.

True _____   Not true _____   Cannot answer from the reading _____

4. The paper should have a clear opinion on the news it reports.

True _____   Not true _____   Cannot answer from the reading _____

5. The paper should attempt to improve knowledge and to influence opinion.

True _____   Not true _____   Cannot answer from the reading _____

Discuss your answers with the rest of the class. When all the students agree on the answers, continue reading.

CONTINUE READING

The three newspapers described here are quite different in many ways, **16** including size, kinds of readers, and language. They are all good newspapers, however, because they meet the needs of their readers by giving them clear, honest, and useful news and opinion that they can use in their personal, intellectual, political, and business lives.

CHART COMPLETION

Working with a partner, fill in the chart below and on the next page with information about the newspapers described in the reading. Write the information requested or mark *yes* or *no*. Put a question mark if the information is not available.

	Al Ahram	Straits Times	Christian Science Monitor
Number of readers			
Number of pages			
Language			
Read in many countries			
Published in two countries			

(Continued at top of next page)

	Al Ahram	*Straits Times*	*Christian Science Monitor*
International news on first page			
Owned by church			
Poor writing			

NEWSPAPER DESCRIPTION

Bring several different newspapers to class. Working in small groups, answer the following questions about each newspaper. When your group has finished, describe the paper you looked at to the rest of the class.

1. What language or languages is the newspaper written in?
2. Where is the newspaper published?
3. How many copies of the newspaper are printed? (You may be able to find this information in the newspaper if you look hard for it.)
4. How many pages does the newspaper have?
5. How much of the paper is advertising?
6. What is on the front page of the paper?
7. Is the newspaper published daily, weekly, or according to some other schedule? If it is a daily, is it published in the morning or the evening?
8. Does the newspaper contain editorials? If it does, what is the subject of one editorial?
9. What is the most important news story in the paper?
10. How much does the newspaper cost?

VOCABULARY EXERCISE

On the left is a list of words from the reading. The number after the word tells which paragraph the word is in. On the right is a list of definitions. There are more definitions than there are words to define. Write the number of each word in the space before its definition.

1. literate (1)   _____ making people believe

2. characteristics (5)   _____ not wanting change

(Continued at top of next page)

3. selected (5)

4. notices (7)

5. official (8)

6. conservative (10)

7. inform (10)

8. local (11)

9. convincing (12)

10. significance of (14)

11. balanced (14)

12. points of view (14)

_____ opinions or ways of thinking about something

_____ what describes or defines something

_____ tell

_____ taken or chosen

_____ able to read and write

_____ having no opinion

_____ the same weight on both sides

_____ recognized by the government

_____ read by many people

_____ limited to a small area

_____ meaning or importance

_____ announcements or short pieces of information

NEW INFORMATION

Write five pieces of information that you learned from the reading. Compare your list with the lists of two other students. How many different pieces of information did your group come up with? Which group in class had the most pieces of information?

1. _____

2. _____

3. _____

4. _____

5. _____

WORD FORMS

Many of the words you have read in this chapter have several forms. One is the verb or action form. Another is the noun form for the action that is done. A third is the noun form for the person or thing doing the action.

Example:

verb or action	noun for what is done	noun for the person or thing doing the action
advertise	*advertising advertisement*	*advertiser*

Fill in the following chart with the other forms of the words given.

verb or action	noun for what is done	noun for the person or thing doing the action
		announcer
		broadcaster
		communicator
	copy	
		editor
	printing	
read		
report		
write		

CHAPTER REVIEW

In this chapter you have read about the development of television, the invention of the photocopy machine, myths that are printed in newspapers, and three good newspapers from around the world. Answer the following questions about the readings. Work alone and answer for yourself. Most of the questions do not have one correct answer; the answers are your opinion or are true for you. When you are finished, discuss your answers with your instructor and the rest of the class.

1. Which reading did you learn the most from? Why?

_____

_____

2. Write five pieces of information that you learned from reading this chapter:

a. _____

_____

b. _____

_____

c. _____

_____

d. _____

_____

e. _____

_____

3. Which reading was the most interesting? Why?

_____

_____

4. Which reading was the easiest to read? Why?

_____

_____

(Continued on next page)

5. Which reading was the most difficult to read? Why?

_____

_____

6. Which reading or readings would probably appear in a magazine or newspaper?

_____

_____

7. Which reading or readings would probably appear in a book?

_____

_____

Now that you have read and thought about news and information, write three questions that you have about the topic.

Example:
What is the best way to get international news in the United States?

1. _____

2. _____

3. _____

Working in groups or as a class, agree on three questions that you think are the most interesting. Then, as a group, decide where you might find the answers to these questions. You might need to look in a particular book or encyclopedia, or interview a particular person. If there is time, go as a group and find the answers to the questions.

WRITING OR SPEAKING SUMMARY

Using the information and language you have learned in this chapter, do one of the following:

1. Your instructor will divide the class into several groups. In your group, choose something that happened recently in your school or area. Collect as much information as you can about the event and write a newspaper story about it. When you are finished, give the story to another group for editing. The editors will then give the stories to the instructor or another group of students to put into a newspaper.

2. Follow the instructions given for the preceding activity, but write the story as a news broadcast. Each group will pick one person to be the reporter and read the story. When you write your news story, write some questions to ask other students to see if they understand the story.

3. When people give news about other people that they do not know is true, or that the person concerned would not like others to know, we say they are _gossiping,_ and the news they communicate is called _gossip._ Some gossip is true, and some is not. You have probably heard gossip about someone you know.

Write, or prepare to give orally, a short story describing some news you heard about another person and how you found out that the news was not true.

4. One invention that can help news travel faster is the television-telephone, a telephone that sends pictures of the speaker at the same time the speaker is talking.

The television-telephone was invented many years ago, but few people want to use it.

Write one page giving your opinions about the television-telephone. Do you think it is a good idea or a bad one? Why?

READING JOURNAL

List the outside reading you did while studying this chapter. (Include the title or type of material, length, topic or subject, and where you found the material.)

_____

_____

_____

Write a journal entry for this outside reading. Your instructor will want to look at your journal and may ask you to tell the rest of the class about something you read. In your journal you might answer the following questions. Or you can write about anything else you felt or learned as you were reading.

What was the most interesting thing you read? Why was it interesting?

What was the least interesting thing you read? Why was it not interesting?

What is one piece of information you learned about news or information from your outside reading?

Was the reading you did difficult or easy? Why do you think it was difficult or easy?

Do you have questions about news or information that you can find the answers to by reading? What are they? What can you read to find the answers?

Did you enjoy the outside reading you did while you studied this chapter? Why or why not?

3

GETTING RICH, GETTING POOR

A penny saved is a penny earned.
—Benjamin Franklin

INTRODUCTION

The sentence at the top of this page was written by a famous American, Benjamin Franklin. Working in pairs or in small groups, write a short explanation of what the sentence means. You might need to ask your instructor or another English speaker for help. Try to make your explanation as clear and as correct as you can.

When you are finished, read your group's explanation to the rest of the class. As a class, try to decide which explanation is the clearest and most correct.

VOCABULARY INTRODUCTION

Below are some words that are related to the subject of money. Work with a group of other students in the class and see if you know what these words mean. If you do not know, ask other students, ask your instructor, or look in a dictionary to find out what they mean. Write the definition of each word you did not know on the blank lines at the top of the next page.

bank	earn	price
borrow	expensive	rich
buy	interest	save
check	loan	spend
coin	million	wealthy
cost	owe	
credit	pay	

DEFINITIONS OF WORDS YOU DID NOT KNOW:

1. _____

2. _____

3. _____

4. _____

5. _____

6. _____

7. _____

8. _____

Working with the other students in your group, think of ten other words that are related to money. When you are finished, you or your instructor can write the words that the class thought of on the blackboard.

_____   _____   _____

_____   _____   _____

_____   _____   _____

_____

Write on the lines below any word written on the blackboard that you are not sure you know the meaning of.

_____   _____   _____

_____   _____   _____

_____   _____   _____

Review these words as you complete this chapter.

OUTSIDE READING

Doing outside reading about money and finance will help you to understand this chapter better. Encyclopedias and almanacs are good sources

College Department

ST. MARTIN'S PRESS
175 Fifth Avenue
New York, N.Y. 10010

PACKING SLIP

Desk Or Examination Copies for

MS. BARBARA EVANS   848478 1 111
HARTNELL COLLEGE   28400 031392

QTY.	NUMBER AND TITLE
01	012594 READING TOGETHER
01	012616 -MANUAL FOR READING TOGETHER

Your comments on our books help us estimate printing requirements, assist us in preparing revisions, and guide us in shaping future books to your needs. Will you please take a moment to fill out and return this postpaid card?

☐ you may quote me for advertising purposes

I   ☐ will adopt   ☐ have adopted   ☐ am seriously considering it

Course title _____ Enrollment_____

Comments
_____
_____
_____
_____
_____
_____
_____
_____
_____

Fold, tape, and mail

of basic information about money in different countries. Many news and business magazines and newspapers also have information about money. Take a few minutes in class and suggest outside readings about money and where to find them. Write on the lines below some good suggestions that you hear.

_____

_____

_____

_____

_____

Be sure to write about your outside reading in your Reading Journal.

INFORMATION GATHERING

Step 1

Make a list of two or three fairly expensive items that you would like to have. Then, with three or four other students, make one list from all your individual lists. Discuss the value of these items and rank them according to how much the group would like to have them. Group members can give any reasons they wish. Decide on one item the group would like to buy.

Step 2

Find out the price of the item the group decided on. Identify a job that one of you has and how much per hour the job pays. If none of you has a job, the instructor can supply an average hourly pay rate for the type of work students such as you can do. Working together, calculate how many hours one of you would have to work to be able to buy the item you want.

Step 3

Present your group's results to the rest of the class. Identify the item you want to buy, why you want it, and how long one of you would have to work to be able to purchase it. The instructor or a student can keep a chart of the planned purchases on the blackboard and note which group would have to work the longest and which the shortest amount of time.

S H O R T   R E A D I N G

PREREADING ACTIVITY

Look at the title of the reading that follows, and try to answer these questions:

1. What do you think the reading will be about?

_____

2. What kind of information might be included in the reading?

_____

_____

Now read the following questions. After you read the questions, work with a partner and write three more questions that you think will be answered in the reading.

1. Is it true that all coins in India are square?
2. Is Japan the only country that has coins with holes in them?
3. Is the United States the only country that does not have paper money in different colors?
4. What metals were used to make coins before the present century?
5. What metals are used to make coins now? Why?
6. What is replacing paper money now? Why?

7. _____

8. _____

9. _____

Read the passage carefully and try to find the answers to the questions.

Money: What Does It Look Like, and What Is It Made Of?

When we think of money, we usually think of currency, or metal coins and paper bills. In the modern world, almost every country and every person uses coins and paper money to exchange for other objects of value. The sizes and shapes of coins are different in various countries, and the size and color of paper money also vary. In India, for example, some coins have square sides. In Japan, coins have holes in the center. In the United States, all paper money is the same size and the same color; only the printing on the bills is different. Most other countries have various sizes and colors for different values of paper money.

Until the twentieth century, most coins were made of precious metals such as gold and silver, or they contained at least some gold or silver. By the middle of the twentieth century, all coins that were actually being used had no gold or silver and were made of less expensive metals, such as copper or aluminum.   **2**

Paper money has replaced metal money for most purposes, and now paper money is being replaced by paper checks, plastic credit cards, and even electronic messages. If this continues, we may soon find that we will not use money at all, but only a series of numbers in computers to buy and sell goods and services.   **3**

QUESTIONS

Now write your answers to the questions from the beginning of the reading, including your own questions. Try to answer from memory. If you cannot remember, go back to the reading and look for the answers. You may not be able to answer all the questions from the reading. Indicate which questions cannot be answered from the reading.

1. Is it true that all coins in India are square?

_____

2. Is Japan the only country that has coins with holes in them?

_____

3. Is the United States the only country that does not have paper money in different colors?

_____

4. What metals were used to make coins before the present century?

_____

5. What metals are used to make coins now? Why?

_____

6. What is replacing paper money now? Why?

_____

(Continued at top of next page)

7. _____

8. _____

9. _____

FILL-IN-THE-BLANK

Working with another student, fill in as many of the blanks as you can in the following passage. For many of the blanks, more than one answer will be possible or correct, but put only one word in each blank. Look carefully at the sentences that come before and after the blank to be sure that the word you choose has meaning in both the sentence and the paragraph and that the form of the word is correct for that sentence. Discuss with your partner any differences in the words you choose, your understanding of the sentences, and your reasons for choosing certain words. The purpose of the exercise is to try to find as many words that can fit in the blanks as possible.

When you and your partner have finished, your instructor will ask you to compare your answers with the answers that your classmates gave. Your instructor may ask you to write your words on the blackboard. Be ready to explain why you chose a word and what the word means. Also be ready to change your answer if other students found a better word. Write other good answers that you hear below the ones that you gave.

Money

Money. Almost everyone wants more of it, and everyone is unhappy when he or

she does not have it. Money has become the universal interest in our lives. People who

have a lot of money may be _____, but they are often also unhappy.
                                    (1)

People who have very little _____ are _____, but, we like to
                               (2)   (3)

think, are still content. Even so, most of us would like to be _____ some
                                                                (4)

day.

One way to become rich is to earn money but not _____ it. Many rich
                                                    (5)

people in the world became rich by _____ most of the money they earned.
                                      (6)

Another way to become rich is to _____ money or to get it from people
                                    (7)

who have died with a lot of money. A third way to become rich is to be lucky and

_____ or _____ money.
     (8)   (9)

Actually, most of us do not want to become rich; we just want enough money to

be able to _____ what we think is important. A house, _____,
         (10)   (11)

some entertainment, and transportation are what we usually spend money on.

Most of us _____ money by working. We work every day, and we are
            (12)

_____ at the end of the day, the week, or the month.
   (13)

If we are lucky, after we pay our _____, we have a little left over to put
                                    (14)

in the _____ and save.
    (15)

LONG READING 1

PREREADING ACTIVITY

What does it mean to be rich? How do you know when you are rich?

There are many ways to answer these questions. Some people answer with amounts of money. Others say you can be rich in ways that have nothing to do with money, like having a close family.

Working with other students in your class, decide on a definition of *rich*. You can express your definition in money or in any other terms. When you are finished, share your definition with the rest of the class. The class will vote on the best one. Write that definition on the lines below.

_____

_____

_____

Now, working as a class, suggest five ways that a person can get rich.

1. _____

2. _____

3. _____

4. _____

5. _____

When you are finished, read the following passage quickly (about five to ten minutes). See how many of the ways that your class suggested are in the reading.

Getting Rich

There are at least four ways to get rich: winning money, earning money, **1** inheriting money, or stealing money. By rich, we mean having enough money so you never have to work for money again, if you do not want to.

Winning money seems easy, but it really is not, and it often does not make you **2** really rich. There are several ways to win money: betting or gambling, lotteries, and contests. Many countries have lotteries in which it is possible to win enough money to become rich, and many people have become rich winning a lottery. But you would have to be very lucky to win a lottery because so many other people are also trying to win and your chances are very small, often one in many million.

Earning money is the hardest way to get rich because it means you have to **3** work, and you usually have to work hard or be especially talented or lucky or both. People who work regular jobs, such as taxi drivers, do not get rich, even if they save all of their money. That is because they do not make enough money during their lifetimes to be able to save enough. They may have more money than their friends and co-workers, but they are not really rich.

A few rich men and women have earned their money, usually by inventing **4** something unusual or popular or by taking chances and being lucky. Sam Walton is one of the richest men in the United States. He is not from a rich family, and he had to deliver newspapers to pay his way through college. He started building small department stores that sold inexpensive items, and he quickly expanded them into a national chain of stores called Wal-Mart.

Most of the really rich people in the world have inherited some or all of their **5** money. Over one third of the richest people in the United States inherited their money from their parents or their spouses. Other rich people are rich because of a combination of inheriting money and earning it. Some heads of government are rich because their countries and families are rich and they have used their money and their position to make more money.

The richest person in the world is probably Sir Mudo Hassanal Bolkiah, the **6** Sultan of Brunei, a small country in Southeast Asia. Brunei gets almost all of its income from oil, and with a population of only about 200,000 people and a cash reserve of over $30 billion, each citizen of Brunei has a very high income.

No one knows for certain just how much money the Sultan has, but he did not **7** inherit his money or earn his money, and he did not steal or win it. The Sultan is a special case, because he is a head of state, a ruler. He is also the prime minister and finance minister. The combination of the wealth of the country and the power of the Sultan and his family have combined to make the Sultan the world's wealthiest person. The Sultan, however, is a very shy and secretive person, and little is known about his private life or the exact amount of money he has.

Some people try to get rich by stealing money. We do not know how many people become rich this way because successful criminals usually do not advertise the fact that they stole money and are now rich. They usually choose to live privately and quietly. **8**

A group of men who tried to become rich by stealing money was the group who took part in the Great Train Robbery in England on August 6, 1963. About fifteen men took part in the robbery of a mail train, and they got away with about $7 million in cash (2,631,684 British pounds). After they divided it, each man got about $150,000. Eventually all of the men were caught and put in jail, although much of the money they got was spent or lost. **9**

One of the men, Ronald Biggs, became famous because, although he was arrested for the crime, he escaped from jail and ran away to Australia. He lived there with his wife and children for four years until he was discovered. He then ran away to Brazil, and the British police were not able to get him out of Brazil. Biggs never got to use much of the money he stole. Much of it he spent trying to get out of England, and the rest he left behind. After leaving England, he lived mostly on money that he earned from working at many different jobs, including house painting. For this famous criminal, trying to get rich by stealing money was not successful. **10**

COMPARISON

Compare the ways of getting rich that the class suggested with the ways mentioned in the reading. Did you find the same ways? If not, how were they different?

COMPREHENSION QUESTIONS

Read the passage again more slowly (about twenty minutes). When you are finished, answer the following questions. Look back at the reading to make sure you have answered correctly. Be able to identify where in the reading you found each answer.

1. How much money do you need to be rich?

_____

2. Why is it difficult to win money in a lottery?

_____

(Continued at top of next page)

3. How did Sam Walton earn money to pay for college?

_____

4. How many rich people in the United States inherited their money?

_____

5. Why is the Sultan of Brunei so rich?

_____

6. Why do we not know exactly how much money the Sultan of Brunei has?

_____

7. Why do we not know how many successful criminals there are?

_____

8. What was the Great Train Robbery?

_____

9. How many men stole money in the Great Train Robbery?

_____

10. What countries did Ronald Biggs live in after he left England?

_____

VOCABULARY EXERCISE

Circle the best answer.

1. In paragraphs 1 and 5 you read the word _inheriting_. The best meaning for _inheriting_ in those paragraphs is:

   a. getting a gift from someone   c. giving to someone

   b. getting from someone who dies   d. borrowing

2. In paragraph 4 you read the phrase _national chain of stores_. The best meaning for this phrase is:

   a. stores found in only one country   c. stores with the name "National Chain"

   b. stores that sell one kind of   d. stores that are located in many parts of
      product   a country

3. In paragraph 5 you read the word *position*. The best meaning for *position* in that paragraph is:

a. level or place in society or government

c. place where someone works

b. place where someone lives

d. place where someone wants to go

4. In paragraph 7 you read the word *secretive*. The best meaning for *secretive* in that paragraph is:

a. working for someone else

c. not giving much information

b. powerful

d. untruthful

5. In paragraph 10 you read the word *arrested*. The best meaning for *arrested* in that paragraph is:

a. caught by the police

c. punished

b. well-known

d. stopped from moving

NEW INFORMATION

Write five pieces of information that you learned from the reading. Compare your list with the lists of two other students. How many different pieces of information did your group come up with? Which group in class had the most pieces of information?

1. _____

2. _____

3. _____

4. _____

5. _____

GROUP WORK: GETTING RICH

Working with the rest of the class, answer the following questions about getting rich:

1. What ways to win money are available in the area where you live?

_____

_____

_____

(Continued at top of next page)

2. What kind of work could you do to become rich? (Make a list of ten kinds of work on the blackboard.)

_____

_____

_____

3. Do you think it is possible for many people to do what Sam Walton did? If yes, how? If not, why not?

_____

_____

_____

4. Do you think it is necessary for leaders of countries to be rich? Why or why not? (You might organize a debate about this.)

_____

_____

_____

5. There is an expression in English, "Crime does not pay." What does this expression mean? Did crime "pay" for Ronald Biggs? Why or why not? Do you think crime generally "pays" for most criminals?

_____

_____

_____

6. Would you like to be rich? If so, which of the four ways of getting rich that are described in the reading would you prefer? Why?

_____

_____

_____

_____

GROUP WORK: BEING RICH

List three things you would do if you were rich:

1. _____

2. _____

3. _____

Now, work with a group of other students. Decide on the three best suggestions from the lists that the students in the group have made. Then write your group's list on the blackboard and compare it with the lists of the other groups in the class. Be prepared to argue for your group's choices. Then vote on which list the class thinks is the best.

L O N G   R E A D I N G   2

PREREADING ACTIVITY

Getting money is sometimes easy. Keeping money can be much more difficult. Some people have no difficulty saving money and always have money to use for an emergency (like medical bills) or to spend on something special (like a new car, a business opportunity, or a vacation). Others seem to be unable to keep much of the money they get. Working as a class, list ten ways that might help you or others to save money.

1. _____

2. _____

3. _____

4. _____

5. _____

6. _____

7. _____

8. _____

9. _____

10. _____

Now, read the following selection carefully, taking about twenty minutes.

Saving Money

(The author of this selection is Rodger Whitehouse, a computer programmer and technical expert. He lives and works in Houston, Texas. He is married and has three children, a house, two cars, and a boat. His salary last year was over $60,000. His wife does not work outside the home.)

Are you any good at saving money? I am not. No matter what I do to try to   1
save money, at the end of every month I have spent everything I earned.

The only time I was able to save money was when I was working as a **2** technician for Royal Dutch Shell, an oil company, in the Middle East. I was only in the Middle East for six months, so I did not get to know many people. Without friends, I had no one to go out with and spend money. I was not married then. Also, because I did not live there permanently, I had very little to buy for myself. The company I worked for supplied me with all my basic needs: a house, a car, medical help if I needed it, and a daily amount for food. They were paying me about $6,000 a month in salary, but they sent that directly to my bank in Houston. By the time I had come back to the United States, I had over $30,000 in the bank.

That $30,000 really helped me to get where I am now. As soon as I got home **3** from the Middle East, I met my wife, Terry, and married her six months later. Right after that, I took $10,000 of my savings and used it as a down payment on a house, not the house I am living in now. The price of the house was $55,000, so I had to borrow the difference. Banks were charging a lot of interest in those days, that was around 1982, so I had to pay over 10 percent a year to the bank for the money I had borrowed.

But I was careful with the rest of the money I had saved. Half of it I put into a **4** long-term savings account that paid me over 11 percent interest a year. With the other half I bought some stocks in some electric companies. Five years later, my $10,000 savings account had grown to more than $16,000, and if you know what happened to the value of stock during that time, you know that my other $10,000 increased a lot too. I have been careful, and I have not spent any of my savings. I know I will need it for the future if I ever lose my job, and I will definitely need it when my children go to college.

Last year I sold my $55,000 house for $75,000 and put the extra money I **5** made down on a much more expensive house. Now that I have a family, I need the larger house. My three children, Bill, Karen, and Jeffrey, each have their own bedroom, and I have a bigger garage for my two cars, a Ford and a Mercedes-Benz. The payments on my house are about $750 a month, and I borrowed money to pay for the cars. Those loans cost me a total of almost $700 a month. As you can see, I like expensive cars.

I am not sure where the rest of my money goes every month. After taxes and **6** payments, we seem to have only about $1,500, and food and clothing for five people and travel and entertainment quickly use that up. We really do like to travel and go boating and picnicking with the children. So at the end of the month, I always seem to be just ready for the next paycheck. I am glad that I have the money that I saved when I worked in the Middle East because I do not seem to be able to save much now. Maybe if I get a raise next year, I can put the extra money in the bank every month.

COMPREHENSION QUESTIONS

Answer the following questions about the reading. Then discuss your answers with the rest of the class or with several other students until you agree on the answers.

1. How was Rodger first able to save money?

_____

2. How much money did he save?

_____

3. What did he do with the money he had saved?

_____

4. How much money did Rodger borrow to buy his first house?

_____

5. About how much interest did Rodger's savings pay him every year?

_____

6. How much cash did Rodger pay when he bought his second house?

_____

7. What is the total of Rodger's house and car payments?

_____

8. About how much money does Rodger earn every month after he pays taxes to the government?

_____

9. How much does Rodger save from his paycheck every month?

_____

10. Is the money that Rodger has saved increasing?

_____

PROBLEM SOLVING: GIVING ADVICE

Before you read about Rodger Whitehouse you made a list of ways to save money. Now that you have read about Rodger, look at your lists again and, working in groups, agree on two or three specific changes that Rodger can make to begin to save money. You can use suggestions from your first list or make new suggestions.

When you are finished, your instructor will list all of the groups' answers on the blackboard. How many different kinds of advice did the class have for Rodger and his family? As a class, decide on the best advice.

VOCABULARY EXERCISE

1. In paragraph 2 there is a word that means "not changing" or "without end." Write that word here:

_____

Write the word that means the opposite of that word here:

_____

2. In paragraph 3 there is a word that means "money charged to use borrowed money." Write that word here:

_____

3. In paragraph 3 there is a noun phrase that means "money paid first as part of the price of something," and in paragraph 5 there is a verb phrase that means "paid the first part of the price." Write those words here:

_____

_____

4. In paragraph 6 there is a word that means "something we do because we enjoy it." Write that word here:

_____

5. In paragraph 6 there is a word that means "an increase in money earned for working." Write that word here:

_____

Discuss your answers with other students until you agree on the correct words.

SUMMARY WRITING

Write a five- to ten-sentence summary of the reading. Include the most important idea first and the other main ideas after the most important one. When you have written your summary, compare it with the summary that another student wrote and answer the following questions:

1. Do you both have the same most important idea? If not, what is different?

_____

_____

Which of you has written the best main idea? Write the best main idea here:

_____

2. What information did you include that your partner did not? _____

_____

What information did your partner include that you did not?_____

_____

Revise your summary so that it includes only the most important idea and the most important other information.

L O N G   R E A D I N G   3

PREREADING ACTIVITY

Another way to get money is to borrow it. Borrowing money is not a way to get rich, because the money must be paid back to the person or company it was borrowed from. Like many Americans, Rodger Whitehouse borrowed money to buy his house. He had to pay extra money, or *interest,* to use the money.

Interest is usually described as the percentage of the borrowed money that we have to pay every year. For example, if we borrow $100 and have to pay 10 percent simple interest, that means that we have to pay $10 for every year that we use the $100. If we use the $100 for one year and then pay it back, we have to pay $110. But often when we borrow money, we pay some of it back every month. Then we want to know the monthly rate of interest. Usually, we can calculate that by dividing the yearly rate by 12. At 10 percent a year, we will pay 10/12, or .83 percent a month. For $100, that would be 83 cents.

Yearly: $100 $\times$ .10 = $10
Monthly: $10 $\div$ 12 (months) = $.83 per month

Calculate the yearly and monthly interest for the following amounts:

Amount	Interest Rate	Yearly Interest	Monthly Interest
Example:			
$100	15%	$15	$1.25
$500	18%	_____	_____
$250	20%	_____	_____
$2000	14%	_____	_____
$1000	14%	_____	_____
$1000	18%	_____	_____

Compare your answers with the answers given by other students in the class. Did you all get the same answers?

The following reading is about credit cards. Credit cards allow you to buy goods or services without using cash. However, you will often have to pay interest if you use the cards.

Before you begin reading, look at the following questions. Then scan the reading to find the answers.

1. What is the writer's general attitude toward using credit cards?

_____

_____

2. The reading contains some specific figures or amounts of money to explain its points. What are they?

_____

_____

3. The reading contains an example of some people who use credit cards. What are their names?

_____

_____

Plastic Poison

How would you feel if someone offered you a card that you could take into a   1
store and buy anything you wanted? You could buy a television or new furniture

or clothing that was worth up to $1,000 or $1,500 or even $2,000. All you would have to do is to sign your name and take what you wanted out of the store.

Three or four weeks later you would get a bill in the mail, but you would not **2** have to pay the whole bill. If you had bought $500 worth of clothes, for example, you would not have to pay $500 but only $10 or $15, and you could pay that $10 or $15 every month.

If you are like most Americans, you would feel that this was a good idea. You **3** would take the card, and you would use it. You would make all kinds of purchases and take a long time to pay for them. Over 75 percent of all Americans have cards such as this.

There is one problem with the cards—they can be financial poison. These **4** cards are just like the poisons we use on insects. If we use them carefully, they can be helpful; but if use them too much, they can kill us. These cards can kill us financially just like a real poison can kill your body.

The cards are called credit cards. They are made of plastic and are about **5** 3 3/8 inches by 2 1/8 inches (8.6 cm by 5.4 cm). The cards have the user's name on them and a number that belongs to the user. They also have the name of the company that gave or issued the card to the user.

A credit card can be useful, as we will see. But credit cards can be poison **6** because it is very easy to continue to use them even when we do not have the money to pay for what we buy. There is one other reason the cards are dangerous. The companies that issue them also charge the user to use the card. For any money that the user does not pay each month (the user's debt) the company charges a percentage of that amount in interest. If you owe the company $500 and do not pay it that month, the company adds from $6 to $8.50 to the $500. Then you owe from $506 to $508.50. The interest is added every month, so a bill that is not paid gets bigger and bigger.

The average family in the United States now has about seven credit cards, **7** and the average debt for each family is over $1,500. Over 10 percent of the families in the United States are "overextended." That is, they have more debt on their credit cards than they can comfortably pay. The amount of debt that is due on credit cards increased almost three times from 1983 to 1988.

What do families spend that money on? Credit cards can be used for all kinds **8** of everyday purchases such as gasoline, food, travel, appliances, books, almost anything that money can buy. In the last few years some new possibilities for spending money with credit cards have emerged. The cards can now be used to pay library fines in Denver if you keep your books too long. They can be used to pay income tax to the U.S. government. They can be used to pay tuition at some schools and colleges. And they can be used, in some places, to pay for funerals.

For some credit card users, a funeral may be the only solution to the debt **9** problems they have caused for themselves by using credit cards. The following story is not a true one, but what happened to the Cathcarts has happened to many real people.

Ellen and Ron Cathcart both work. He is a manager in a large retail store, and **10** she is an architect. Last year they earned over $65,000, but they also used their credit cards and bought $23,000 worth of goods and services. They took vacations to Hawaii, bought a lot of expensive clothes, and often went out to dinner. They always used their credit cards and thought that they would have no difficulty paying for what they had bought. Ellen and Ron now have monthly bills of $735 just to make the minimum payments on their credit cards. When this amount is added to their other bills, they have nothing left over to save or to pay off the credit card bills more quickly. At that rate, it will take over three years to pay off their credit card debt if they do not add any more to it.

The Cathcarts went to see a credit counselor, a person who helps people who   **11** have too much debt. What the credit counselor told the Cathcarts first was that they needed "plastic surgery," not the kind that makes us look better but the kind that makes us spend better. They took a pair of scissors and cut all their credit cards into pieces. Now they pay cash for everything, and they have much better control over what they spend. It will take them several years to pay off the debts they built up with their credit cards, but they are certain that they will not make the same mistake again.

To many other people, however, credit cards are not poison but a   **12** convenience. With credit cards, we do not have to carry a lot of cash, we can order what we need over the telephone, we can pay for airplane tickets immediately, and we can use the credit intelligently to pay for expenses such as furniture and vacations. As long as we are careful to keep our spending under control and are able to pay for what we buy without building up large debts, credit cards will not be a problem but a benefit.

COMPREHENSION QUESTIONS

Read the selection again, slowly this time (about twenty minutes). When you are finished, answer the following questions:

1. Do most credit card companies require the user to pay all the money they owe every month?

_____

2. About how much interest do the credit card companies charge?

_____

3. How much money does the average American family owe on each credit card it has?

_____

(Continued at top of next page)

4. Did debt on credit cards increase or decrease during the first part of the 1980s?

_____

5. What are some unusual items that can be paid for with credit cards?

_____

6. About what percentage of their income did the Cathcarts spend using their credit cards?

_____

7. What does a credit counselor do?

_____

8. What is "plastic surgery" in the reading?

_____

GROUP WORK: USING CREDIT CARDS

Work with another student or with a group of students and make a plan for using credit cards. Start to plan by trying to answer the following questions:

1. What would you like to spend money on using the cards?
2. What would not be good to spend money on using the cards?
3. How will you find the money to pay the bills you get from using the cards?
4. How long will it take you to pay for using the cards?

When you are finished, present your plan orally to the class or write your plan and give it to your instructor.

VOCABULARY EXERCISE

On the left is a list of words from the reading. The number after the word tells which paragraph the word is in. On the right is a list of definitions. There are more definitions than there are words to define. Write the number of each word in the space before its definition.

1. bill (2)   _____ the least or smallest amount

2. purchases (3)   _____ common, ordinary, not special

(Continued at top of next page)

3. issued (5)   _____ ceremony when someone dies

4. percentage (6)   _____ the most or greatest amount

5. everyday (8)   _____ paper saying that we owe money for something
                                 we bought or used

6. appliances (8)

7. funeral (9)   _____ what we buy

8. minimum (10)   _____ a prize in a contest

9. pay off (10)   _____ to pay all of a loan

10. convenience (12)   _____ given by a company

                           _____ part of a whole

                           _____ machines used for housework

                           _____ something that is easy

PROBLEM SOLVING

Gerry Madison is going away for the summer to work in a national park. Gerry's mother wants him to get a credit card to use to pay for his expenses as he travels and works. Gerry's father does not want him to have a credit card and believes that Gerry will be fine without one. Divide into groups representing each point of view. In your group, think of as many reasons as you can why Gerry should or should not have the card. When all the groups are finished, each group should write its three best reasons on the blackboard. As a class, vote on whether or not Gerry should get the card. Or have a class debate to decide if Gerry should get the card.

OPTIONAL APPLICATION ACTIVITIES
Budget Planning

Work in a group or with one other student, and imagine that you are a family with an income of $27,000 a year. Your family consists of a husband, a wife, and two children, four and seven years old. Make a monthly budget for your family. Decide how much you will spend on the following eight items. Describe your budget to the rest of the class, and be able to give reasons for your decisions.

Housing _____

Food _____

Clothing _____

Recreation and entertainment _____

Transportation _____

Telephone _____

Savings _____

Other (list) _____

Salaries

Working with other students, guess the average salary for people with the following jobs in the country where you are studying. When all the groups are finished, compare answers and note the highest and lowest guesses. Then try to find out what the actual average salary is. Your instructor might be able to help you find this information.

	Your guess	Highest guess	Lowest guess	Actual salary
Schoolteacher				
Airline pilot				
Taxi driver				
Medical doctor				
Construction worker (carpenter or concrete worker)				
Secretary				
Waiter or waitress				
Police officer				

CROSSWORD PUZZLE

Fill in the crossword puzzle on page 91 with words related to money.

ACROSS

1. The amount we have to pay to buy something.
5. Most of us like to _____ money.
8. A very large number.
9. Small, metal form of money.
12. Teachers usually do not _____ a lot of money.
13. His _____ is less than $20,000 a year.
15. What we have to pay to the government.
16. The money of the United States.
17. What this chapter is about.

DOWN

2. Something that costs a lot of money is _____.
3. What we need to have to earn money.
4. He earns the same _____ every week no matter how many hours he works.
6. A safe place to keep money.
7. An easy way to get money.
10. If you have not paid for something you still _____ money.
11. A valuable metal.
14. The hardest thing to do with money.

CHAPTER REVIEW

In this chapter you have read about what money looks like, different ways of getting rich, the difficulties of saving money, and the dangers of credit cards. Answer the following questions about the readings. Work alone and answer for yourself. Most of the questions do not have one correct answer; the answers are your opinion or are true for you. When you are finished, discuss your answers with your instructor and the rest of the class.

1. Which reading did you learn the most from? Why?

_____

_____

(Continued at top of next page)

2. Write five pieces of information that you learned from the readings in this chapter:

a. _____

_____

b. _____

_____

c. _____

_____

d. _____

_____

e. _____

_____

3. Which reading was the most interesting? Why?

_____

_____

4. Which reading was the easiest to read? Why?

_____

_____

5. Which reading was the most difficult to read? Why?

_____

_____

Now that you have read and thought about money, write three questions that you still have about the topic.

Example:
How much does it cost a year to live in Tokyo? _____

1. _____

2. _____

3. _____

Working in groups or as a class, agree on three questions that you think are the most interesting. Then, as a group, decide where you might find the answers to these questions. You might need to look in a particular book or encyclopedia, or interview a particular person. If there is time, go as a group and find the answers to the questions.

WRITING OR SPEAKING SUMMARY

Choose one of the following topics. Then, using the information and language you have learned in this chapter, write at least one page on that topic or prepare to talk to the class about it.

1. Describe your biggest problem with money and how you plan to solve it. Would a credit card be helpful or harmful? Do you need to make a budget for yourself?
2. Describe how rich you hope to become and how you plan to do it. How will you save or keep your money?
3. How will what you have learned in this chapter change how you use money?

READING JOURNAL

List the outside reading you did while studying this chapter. (Include the title or type of material, length, topic or subject, and where you found the material.)

Write a journal entry for this outside reading. Your instructor will want to look at your journal and may ask you to tell the rest of the class about something you read. In your journal you might answer the following questions. Or you can write about anything else you felt or learned as you were reading.

What was the most interesting thing you read? Why was it interesting?

What was the least interesting thing you read? Why was it not interesting?

What is one piece of information you learned about money from your outside reading?

Was the reading you did difficult or easy? Why do you think it was difficult or easy?

Do you have questions about money that you can find the answers to by reading? What are they? What can you read to find the answers?

Did you enjoy the outside reading you did while you studied this chapter? Why or why not?

Chapter
4

FOOD,
GLORIOUS FOOD

You are what you eat.
—Victor Lindlahr

INTRODUCTION

The expression at the top of this page is often heard in discussions about food. Working with one or more other students, try to decide what this expression means. Compare your answer with the answers of other groups in the class. Ask several speakers of English and see if they agree.

Once you have decided on a meaning, discuss the meaning with the students in your group and decide if you agree with the expression. Be ready to tell the rest of the class what you have decided and why.

VOCABULARY INTRODUCTION

Below are some words that are related to the subject of food. Work with a group of students in the class and see if you know what these words mean. If you do not know, ask other students, ask your instructor, or look in a dictionary to find out what the words mean. Write the definition of each word you did not know.

bean	meal	taste
cook	mineral	tomato
egg	oil	vegetable
flour	pasta	vitamin
health	protein	

DEFINITIONS OF WORDS YOU DID NOT KNOW:

1. _____

2. _____

3. _____

4. _____

5. _____

6. _____

7. _____

8. _____

Working with other students in your group, write on the lines below ten other words that are related to food. When you are finished, you or your instructor can write the words that the class thought of on the blackboard.

_____   _____   _____

_____   _____   _____

_____   _____   _____

_____

Write on the lines below any word written on the blackboard that you are not sure you know the meaning of.

_____   _____   _____

_____   _____   _____

_____   _____   _____

Review these words as you complete this chapter.

OUTSIDE READING

While you read this chapter, it will be helpful if you do outside reading about food and nutrition. Magazines often have articles about food, cooking, and agriculture. Even if you do not cook, cookbooks have interesting and useful information about food. Newspapers in the United States usually have a section about buying and cooking food. These newspapers also have advertisements for food stores that give names, prices, and often pictures of various foods.

Take a few minutes in class and suggest outside readings about food and eating and where to find them. Write on the lines below some good suggestions that you hear.

_____

_____

_____

_____

_____

Be sure to write about your outside reading in your Reading Journal.

INFORMATION GATHERING

Most of us like some foods and dislike other foods. But the foods that we like are not always ones that are good for us, and there are often foods that we do not like that are very good for us. In the first column, write the names of three kinds of food you like that are good for you and three you like that are not good for you. In the second column, write the names of three foods you do not like that are good for you and three you do not like or will not eat that are not good for you. Be ready to give your reasons for liking or not liking the foods.

FOODS I LIKE:	FOODS I DO NOT LIKE:
Good for Me	**Good for Me**
_____	_____
_____	_____
_____	_____

(Continued at top of next page)

Bad for Me   **Bad for Me**

_____   _____

_____   _____

_____   _____

When everyone in the class has finished, try to agree on one food that everyone likes and one that no one likes.

S H O R T   R E A D I N G

PREREADING ACTIVITY

Read the following questions and try to answer them. (You will probably not be able to answer all the questions.) Discuss your answers in class. Then read the passage that follows slowly and carefully, taking about ten minutes.

1. Which do you like most to eat—rice, meat, vegetables, or seafood?

_____

2. What is one food that is typical of the United States?

_____

3. How many basic nutrients do our bodies need?

_____

4. What nutrient is common in eggs and meat?

_____

5. What do carbohydrates contribute to nutrition?

_____

6. Why is sugar not a good form of carbohydrate?

_____

7. When does the body use fats as a source of energy?

_____

8. According to the reading, what is the best source of vitamins and minerals?

_____

The Building Blocks of Nutrition

As human beings, with different cultures, habits, and tastes, each of us eats differently from our friends and neighbors and much differently from people in other parts of the world. Some of us eat rice every day. Some of us have never eaten rice. Some of us love to eat meat, or fish and other seafood. Others never, or almost never, eat meat or fish and live almost entirely on vegetables. Each of us has a favorite food, and each country has typical and common dishes and recipes. **1**

Nutrition is the word for what we take into our bodies so we will grow and stay healthy. Whether our food is from animals (beef, pork, mutton), from the sea (fish, shrimp, lobster, shellfish, crab), or from the earth (wheat, corn, green vegetables, fruits), all food is made up of several basic elements or building blocks. Our bodies need basically four types of nutrients from food: proteins, carbohydrates, fats, and vitamins and minerals. Proteins help the body grow and repair itself when it is damaged. They are found in many kinds of food, but especially in eggs, milk, meat, and fish, although many vegetable foods also contain high amounts of protein. **2**

Carbohydrates give us energy. Athletes who are going to be active for a long time often eat large amounts of carbohydrates before competing. The most beneficial carbohydrates come from vegetable sources such as wheat, corn, and beans. Sugars are also a form of carbohydrates, but the body uses them quickly and without much benefit. **3**

Fats also provide energy to the body after the energy from carbohydrates is used up. Fats come from both animal and vegetable sources. **4**

Vitamins and minerals are another group of food elements. There are many vitamins and minerals (vitamins A, B, C, D, and E, and the minerals iron, zinc, iodine, and others) and scientists often disagree about how much of each is necessary. But we do know that the best way to get the vitamins and minerals we need is to eat the right amount of the right kinds of food. Eating right by eating the right amounts of the right combination of food types is the best way to make sure that we get all of the nutrition we need. **5**

Now look again at the questions from the beginning of the reading. In your group or as a class, try to agree on the answers.

FILL-IN-THE-BLANK

Working with another student, fill in the blanks in the following passage. For many of the blanks, more than one answer will be possible or correct, but put only one word in each blank. Look carefully at the sentences that come before and after the blank to be sure that the word you choose has meaning in both the sentence and the paragraph and that the form of the word is correct for that sentence. Discuss with your partner any differences in the words you choose, your understanding of the sentences, and your reasons for choosing certain words. The purpose of the exercise is to try to find as many words that can fit in the blanks as possible.

When you and your partner have finished, your instructor will ask you to compare your answers with the answers that your classmates gave. Your instructor may ask you to write your words on the blackboard. Be ready to explain why you chose a word and what the word means. Also be ready to change your answer if other students found a better word. Write other good answers that you hear below the ones that you gave.

Food

Do you like to eat? That is a funny question. We do not ask people if they like to breath, but we do ask if they like to eat. _____ is as important to life as
                                                            (1)

breathing is. If we stop breathing, we will _____ in a few minutes. If we
                                              (2)

stop _____, we will also die, but it will take longer. If we eat good
       (3)

_____, we will be _____ and our _____ will be free
      (4)   (5)   (6)

from _____.
       (7)

Food comes from two main sources. Much of our food, especially the food we call

vegetables, comes from _____. _____ comes from animals.
                             (8)   (9)

Another important food that comes from animals is _____. Some foods we
                                                        (10)

do not _____; we eat them raw. Other foods we _____ by
            (11)   (12)

boiling, frying, roasting, or baking. _____ is a common baked food that
                                          (13)

many of us eat every day.

In fact, all of this talk about _____ has made me _____! I am
                                      (14)   (15)

going to make myself a _____ with two pieces of bread and some
                             (16)

_____. I bet you would like to have some _____ right now!
      (17)   (18)

L O N G   R E A D I N G   1

PREREADING ACTIVITY

Are there any students in class who do not eat meat? How many? What are their reasons? Do they never eat meat, or do they usually not eat meat?

The following reading is about vegetarians, or people who do not eat meat. As a class, or in groups within the class, make a list of five questions that you would like to have answered about vegetarians.

1. _____

2. _____

3. _____

4. _____

5. _____

Now read the following passage quickly, and try to find the answers to your questions.

A Dietary Minority

All over the world, and for many different reasons, there are millions of people   1
who rarely or never eat meat. These people are called vegetarians. To people
who eat meat, being a vegetarian may seem like a very strange way to live, but
most vegetarians are very happy with their choice of diet. They choose their diets
for several different reasons, and, in fact, there are different kinds of vegetarians.

Some vegetarians eat almost anything except food that actually comes from   2
the killing of live animals. Their diets may or may not include fish and other
seafood, but usually include milk and other dairy products and eggs. Some
vegetarians are only sometimes vegetarians. They eat meat products occasionally, on social and special occasions, but they generally try to avoid doing so. On
the other hand, there are some extreme vegetarians who avoid eating anything
that comes from animals, including milk, cheese, and eggs.

One of the first questions many vegetarians are asked is how they stay   3
healthy. Meat-eaters often believe that meat is such an important source of
protein and vitamins that vegetarians must have difficulty staying healthy. However, only extreme vegetarians, who live on only grains and green vegetables,
seem to have any real health problems. Extreme vegetarians are sometimes
very thin and have a shortage of B-vitamins. Less extreme vegetarians are usually

in better health than most meat-eaters. Recent research is proving that we need less protein than scientists once thought. Young men were once recommended to eat between 50 to 100 grams of protein a day. Recent recommendations from the World Health Organization are between 30 and 40 grams, and many studies show that young men who eat as little as 20 grams of protein a day can be quite healthy. Since many non-meat foods are good sources of protein, it is not difficult for a vegetarian to get as much protein as he or she needs. Combinations of beans and other legumes and cheese and other dairy products are excellent sources of protein. Many traditional vegetarian diets, such as is common in parts of India, are made up of peas or beans and yogurt.

4   In fact, vegetarians have an enormous health advantage. One of the major health problems in modern societies is not too little protein, but too much food, especially in the form of animal fats. Medical evidence suggests that animal fats, including butter, contribute to the development of cholesterol in the human body. High amounts of cholesterol seem to be part of the cause of heart disease. Most vegetarians have low levels of cholesterol. High amounts of animal fats also seem to lead to certain kinds of cancer, and vegetarians typically have less of these cancers than people who eat a lot of meat. Overall, studies comparing the health of vegetarians and meat-eaters show that the meat-eaters are twice as likely to die of heart disease as vegetarians are.

5   Better health is one reason that people choose to become vegetarians. Another reason is religion. Some religions prohibit the eating of meat. The largest of these is the Hindu religion, which has about 600 million believers in the world. Although not all Hindus are vegetarian, many are, and there are many believers of other religions such as Buddhism and even some Christian religions who also do not eat meat.

6   Many vegetarians do not eat meat simply because they do not like the taste of it. They have no religious or philosophical reasons; they just do not like meat. Another important reason that vegetarians give for not eating meat is the health advantages that were given above. Lastly, there are many people who do not eat meat because they just do not like the idea of killing animals for food. They believe that life, all life, is valuable, and that we do not have to destroy life to feed ourselves when there are other good sources of food.

7   There is also an economic argument for vegetarianism; animals are not good sources of food because they use too much land that could be used for growing food plants and they eat plants that could be used for food. For example, a piece of land can produce five times as much protein if rice is grown on it than if the land is used to raise animals for food. Where conditions are right, then, we can produce three to five times as much food by using the land for growing food plants rather than for raising animals.

8   How many vegetarians are there? It is difficult to say, and some vegetarians feel very lonely, especially when they go out to a restaurant with a group of meat-eating friends. But in the United States about 3.5 to 4 percent of the population say that they are vegetarian. In other countries the percentage of vegetarians varies according to the religion and culture and availability of meat.

Who is vegetarian? Vegetarians are found everywhere among people who **9** can choose what they eat. Vegetarianism is not just for some religious groups or those who are very concerned about their health. Many athletes, politicians, artists, and entertainers are vegetarians. Past and present vegetarians include Paul McCartney, one of the members of the musical group known as the Beatles; Mahatma Gandhi; Kenneth Kaunda, the President of Zambia; a number of marathon runners and weight-lifters; and Adolf Hitler.

QUESTIONS

How many of the questions from your list did you find answers to? If there are questions that were not answered in the reading, you might ask the people that you talk to in the survey exercise (see pages 104–5).

FILL-IN-THE-BLANK

Working with a partner or in a small group, fill in the blanks in the following paragraph with information from the reading.

There are _____ kinds of vegetarians. Some _____ eat meat,
    (1)   (2)

and some eat meat only _____. _____ vegetarians are some-
          (3)   (4)

times thin and unhealthy, but most vegetarians are _____ than most people
                (5)

who eat meat. _____ is one reason why people choose to become
      (6)

vegetarian. _____ belief is another important reason. The economic reason
    (7)

for being a vegetarian is that food animals use too much _____. Although
                (8)

vegetarianism is popular, less than _____ percent of the population of the
          (9)

United States is vegetarian.

SUMMARY WRITING

Read the selection again, more carefully this time (about twenty minutes). Take notes as you read. When you are finished, write a short summary of the reading. Your instructor will ask several students to read their summaries to the class. Listen carefully to each summary and decide if it leaves out any important information or includes information that is not in the reading.

SURVEY

Each student should ask five people from outside the class the following questions:

1. Are you a vegetarian?
2. If you are, what is your reason for being a vegetarian?
3. How long have you been a vegetarian?
4. What are two or three foods that you usually eat?

When all the surveys are completed, put together a list of the results.

1. How many people were asked? _____

2. How many of these people are vegetarians? _____

3. What percentage of these people are vegetarian? _____

4. Is that percentage higher or lower than the percentage given in the reading?

_____

5. List the three most common reasons given for being a vegetarian:

_____

_____

_____

6. How many of the reasons given by the people surveyed are the same as the reasons given in the reading? _____ How many are new or different?

_____

7. What is the longest anyone has been a vegetarian? _____

VOCABULARY EXERCISE

On the left is a list of words from the reading. The number after the word tells which paragraph the word is in. On the right is a list of definitions. There are more definitions than there are words to define. Write the number of each word in the space before its definition.

1. diet (1)   _____ something that helps or makes better
2. occasionally (2) _____ never changes
3. extreme (3)   _____ between often and never
4. research (3)   _____ changes
5. major (4)   _____ what we eat
6. evidence (4)   _____ to make possible
7. contribute (4)   _____ careful study
8. prohibit (5)   _____ great in size or importance
9. advantage (6)   _____ far from normal or usual
10. varies (8)   _____ to help happen

                     _____ information that helps prove something

                     _____ to say something cannot be done

DEBATE

Divide the class into two groups or an equal number of groups. Half the students should be "pro-vegetarian" and prepare three reasons why everyone should become a vegetarian. The other half should be "anti-vegetarian" and prepare three reasons why people should not be vegetarian. Have each side present its reasons and give the other side time to answer the arguments.

L O N G   R E A D I N G   2

PREREADING ACTIVITY

Look at the following list and write down what part of the world you think each food came from originally. Work with a partner or in a small group, and try to agree on the answers.

If you do not know what some of the foods are, find out from a classmate or your instructor, or look in a dictionary.

corn (maize) _____

tomatoes _____

pizza _____

noodles _____

apple _____

hamburgers _____

potatoes _____

ice cream _____

sandwich _____

Now read the following selection quickly (about fifteen minutes), looking only for the origins of the foods in the list (not all of the foods in the list will be mentioned).

Where Did They Come From?

In the modern world, transportation and the spread of products have made   1
almost any foods and drinks available all over the world. Americans drink Russian

vodka, and the Japanese eat American beef. But many foods that we eat today originally were eaten or grown in only one part of the world. The origins of various foods are interesting.

Tomatoes, for example, are originally from the Americas. Potatoes are also originally from the Americas. Both foods were first taken to Spain and spread from there to the rest of Europe and, eventually, the rest of the world. Both vegetables are so common all over the world now that it is difficult to imagine they were unknown outside of the Americas only five hundred years ago. **2**

One food that is rapidly spreading throughout the modern world is the hamburger. The hamburger has many variations. The basic hamburger is, of course, made of chopped or ground beef that has been fried and put between two halves of a round roll or bun. It may be eaten plain or with a variety of additions. In modern fast-food shops, hamburgers are sold in what seem like hundreds of varieties. The cheeseburger, a hamburger fried with a slice of cheese on top, is a common variation. Hamburgers are also eaten with many different additions, including lettuce, tomato, mustard, ketchup, pickles, and onions. **3**

As recently as twenty or thirty years ago, the hamburger was a basic food in the United States, Canada, and some European countries, but it was not eaten in many other countries. Now, energetic businesspeople are taking the hamburger to South America, Japan, the Middle East, and China. **4**

Hamburgers have an interesting history. They were made at one time in the German city of Hamburg, but the custom of chopping meat was begun by the Tartars of Central Asia more than a thousand years ago. They chopped the meat of cows because the meat was tough, and they often ate the meat raw. Many centuries later, Russian Tartars carried the custom of eating chopped meat to Germany. Germans began to eat chopped meat also, and in the city of Hamburg, chopped meat was eaten both cooked and raw and became known as "Hamburg steak." **5**

In the late nineteenth century, German immigrants to the United States brought the custom of eating chopped meat steak. By the early part of this century, Americans were eating hamburger steaks between slices of bread and were calling the sandwich a "hamburger." The sandwich quickly spread throughout the United States. In the 1930s and after, many small American restaurants advertised "the best hamburger in town," but it was large companies such as White Castle, McDonalds, Burger King, and Wendy's in the United States and Wimpy's in England that made the hamburger a standard kind of fast food all over the United States and, recently, the world. Hamburgers made by U.S. companies are now sold in Caracas, Venezuela; Beijing, China; Tokyo, Japan; and Moscow, the Soviet Union. **6**

Pasta is an Italian word for a large group of differently shaped foods all made from wheat flour, cut and formed into various shapes, and eaten after being boiled in water and, usually, combined with a sauce. Spaghetti, macaroni, and noodles are all forms of pasta, but pasta, especially in Italy, can have over five hundred shapes and sizes. One pasta-maker in New York claimed that there must be over a thousand forms of pasta. It is not clear where pasta originated. The usual explanation is that noodles were first made in China over three thousand years **7** ago. When Marco Polo, the Italian traveler, returned to Italy from China in the 1300s, he is said to have returned with the idea for making pasta. According to the story, the Italians took the Chinese idea and developed it into the many forms of pasta we have today.

Other historians, however, can show that the Italians were eating a kind of **8** ravioli, or a meat or vegetable filling inside a pasta shell, long before Marco Polo returned from China. So we really do not know if pasta was invented in China and carried to Italy or if it was invented in both places, and probably many more places also. The Chinese still make many kinds of noodle dishes. Italian pasta is famous, and Italian pasta dishes are eaten all over the world. In Afghanistan and Russia, there are people who eat a kind of ravioli called *ashak,* which has a vegetable filling inside a pasta shell.

Italians eat over sixty pounds of pasta per person every year. People in **9** the United States eat only about seven or eight pounds per person. Pasta is good food. It is usually made only from wheat flour and water, although a special, hard wheat is used for the wheat flour. Eggs are added to some kinds of noodles, and in other countries, noodles are made with rice, bean, and other kinds of flour. Pasta has a lot of carbohydrates, and carbohydrates are now thought to be a very important ingredient in human nutrition. Pasta is also low in fat. Since pasta can be cooked and eaten in so many different ways, and because it is eaten in so many different countries, it must be called one of the basic foods of the world.

Sauces are used in cooking almost everywhere. In fact, the word *sauce* **10** almost has no meaning in English because it is used in so many different ways. Sauces are cooked and added to food such as pasta. Sauces may also be uncooked, such as the white mayonnaise that is used on many sandwiches. One simple sauce has become almost universal on dinner tables all over the world; that sauce is ketchup, or catsup (both spellings are common).

Actually, the word for ketchup entered the English language before the sauce **11** that we know today did. The word *ketchup* is from a Chinese word something like *ke-tsiap* that was used to mean "a kind of sauce for food." But *ke-tsiap* did not have any tomatoes in it, and modern ketchup is made mostly of tomatoes.

British sailors liked the kechap sauce they found in Asia and took the idea **12** back home to England. During the 1700s, ketchup was a common sauce used all over England. It still did not contain tomatoes though. It was the Americans who first added tomatoes to the sauce. From 1800 to 1850, the recipe for ketchup changed until it became mostly a tomato sauce and also became a sauce used in almost every American kitchen. Ketchup spread from the United States to many other parts of the world, completing a journey begun many centuries earlier in China.

Types of food, just like ideas and manufactured goods, often begin in one **13** place and spread, often with many changes in form, from one place to another. It is difficult to imagine a world without tomatoes, but it was not long ago that most of the world did not know about this vegetable. Maybe in a few more centuries the hamburger will be as universal as the tomato.

ORIGINS

How many of the foods on the list were mentioned in reading? Did you know where the foods came from? Compare your answers with the following list:

corn (maize) *Americas*

tomatoes *Americas*

pizza *Italy*

noodles *China*

apple *Europe and Asia*

hamburgers *Asia (first), then Germany*

potatoes *Americas*

ice cream *China*

sandwich *England*

Now read the selection again, more slowly this time (about twenty minutes). Then do the following exercises.

INFORMATION IDENTIFICATION

Read the following ten statements. If the information in the statement is mentioned in the reading, write *Y* before the statement. If the information is not mentioned in the reading, write *N* before the statement.

1. _____ *Pasta* is a word that means "paste."

2. _____ Chinese *ke-tsiap* and modern ketchup are very different.

3. _____ Hamburgers are high in protein and fats.

4. _____ There are at least five hundred shapes of pasta.

5. _____ Pasta is over 80 percent carbohydrate.

6. _____ Ketchup contains sugar.

7. _____ Hamburgers are a common food in Hamburg, Germany.

8. _____ Pasta may have been invented in Italy.

9. _____ Ketchup developed its modern form by 1850.

10. _____ Ketchup contains a lot of vitamin C.

FILL-IN-THE-BLANK

Fill in the blanks in the following paragraph with information from the reading.

The reading is about _____ of food. There are three examples in the
(1)

reading. They are _____, _____, and _____. Ham-
(2)   (3)   (4)

burgers come from a way of eating meat originally found in _____ but later
(5)

taken to _____, where the name *hamburger* came from. Hamburgers
(6)

became _____ in the United States in the _____ century. Pasta
(7)   (8)

originally comes from _____ and maybe from _____. It is made
(9)   (10)

from _____ and water and contains a lot of _____. It is made
(11)   (12)

in many different _____. Ketchup developed its modern form in
(13)

_____, but it is based on a _____ originally made in and car-
(14)   (15)

ried home by _____ sailors. Modern ketchup is made mostly of
(16)

_____.
(17)

PARAPHRASE

Below are five sentences taken from the reading. After each sentence are two
other sentences, one of which has approximately the same meaning as the sentence
from the reading. Put a check (√) before the sentence that has the same meaning.

Example: **Both foods were first taken to Spain and spread from there to the rest
of Europe and, eventually, the rest of the world.**

_____ a. **Foods spread from Europe to Spain and to the rest of the world.**

___√___ b. **After reaching Spain, some foods spread to Europe and other parts of
the world.**

1. As recently as twenty or thirty years ago, the hamburger was a basic food in the
United States, Canada, and some European countries, but it was not eaten in many
other countries.

———— a. The hamburger was not a popular food in Asia and South America until recently.

———— b. The hamburger became a basic food in the United States and Europe recently.

2. Spaghetti, macaroni, and noodles are all forms of pasta, but pasta, especially in Italy, can have over five hundred shapes and sizes.

———— a. Spaghetti, macaroni, and noodles are the only forms of pasta in Italy.

———— b. Spaghetti, macaroni, and noodles are only a few of the forms that pasta can have.

3. When Marco Polo, the Italian traveler, returned to Italy from China in the 1300s, he is said to have returned with the idea for making pasta.

———— a. Marco Polo probably brought the idea of pasta to Italy from China.

———— b. Marco Polo returned to Italy to make Chinese pasta.

4. So we really do not know if pasta was invented in China and carried to Italy or if it was invented in both places, and probably many more places also.

———— a. Pasta may have been invented several times and in several places.

———— b. Pasta was definitely invented in both China and Italy.

5. Since pasta can be cooked and eaten in so many different ways, and because it is eaten in so many different countries, it must be called one of the basic foods of the world.

———— a. Pasta is a basic food because it is common.

———— b. Pasta is a basic food because it is healthy.

VOCABULARY EXERCISE

Circle the best answer.

1. In paragraph 2 you read the word *common*. The best meaning for *common* in that paragraph is:

a. inexpensive

b. not good

c. unusual or special

d. usual or found everywhere

(Continued at top of next page)

2. In paragraph 3 you read the word *variations*. The best meaning for *variations* in that paragraph is:

a. similar types

c. sizes

b. different types

d. flavors

3. In paragraph 3 you read the word *plain*. The best meaning for *plain* in that paragraph is:

a. simple, without additions

c. with a lot of extras

b. quickly

d. flat

4. In paragraph 5 you read the word *raw*. The best meaning for *raw* in that paragraph is:

a. full of taste

c. chopped

b. boiled

d. not cooked

5. In paragraph 6 you read the word *standard*. The best meaning for *standard* in that paragraph is:

a. regular, typical, ordinary

c. healthy, nutritious

b. special, unusual, distinctive

d. expensive, costly

6. In paragraph 7 you read the word *originated*. The best meaning for *originated* in that paragraph is:

a. was first sold

c. was first discovered

b. was first made

d. was first grown

7. In paragraph 13 you read the word *imagine*. The best meaning for *imagine* in that paragraph is:

a. think of

c. describe

b. draw a picture of

d. like

L O N G   R E A D I N G   3

PREREADING ACTIVITY

Read the paragraph below. Then answer the questions that follow.

The Magical Mystery Food

What food is eaten in one form or another by people all over the world, is   1
cheap and easy to produce, is extremely healthy, is almost never eaten in its

natural form, is used to make many products that have nothing to do with food, and probably would not be recognized by many people except the farmers who produce it?

Do you know or can you guess what food this paragraph is describing?

_____

How many students in the class think the food comes from an animal?

_____

How many students think it comes from the sea?

_____

How many students think it comes from a plant?

_____

Now read the rest of the passage and find out for certain what this food is and where it comes from. Read slowly, taking about twenty minutes.

There is such a food. No, it is not wheat, although wheat is certainly healthy   2
and common. It is not milk either, since milk is often consumed in exactly the same form as it is produced. And it is not water, although sometimes the food we are talking about seems as common as water. No, the food that is described above is a food that many people who eat it have not even heard of and many more have never even seen. That food is the soybean.

What is the soybean, and why is it so special? Soybeans are a simple bean   3
that is easy to grow. The bean comes in many forms, although the most common is a round shape about 1/4 of an inch (0.6 centimeters) in diameter. Soybeans come in many colors—yellow, black, brown, green, or multicolored—but a tan or light brown color is the most common in modern, cultivated beans. Soybeans do not need fertile soil or a lot of care. The two-feet tall plants grow in many climates, are not subject to many diseases, and are easy to harvest by machine.

The soybean was probably first grown by farmers in China over three   4
thousand years ago. In China and Japan the soybean has been used for centuries as the basis for a simple food, doufu (in China) or tofu (in Japan). Doufu or tofu is soft, white, and almost tasteless. It is made by crushing wet soybeans, mixing the crushed beans with water, straining the water from the beans, and adding salt to the remaining mixture to make the mixture solid. The best doufu is sold and eaten fresh, although it can be preserved for several weeks.

Doufu does not, by itself, have much flavor. It is usually cooked with other   5
foods or combined with sauces. But doufu is very healthy food. It is high in protein and low in almost everything else that is not good for us, such as fat. Fresh doufu

is about 80 percent water, 10 percent protein, 5 percent fat, 3 percent sugar, and 2 percent other elements.

Soybeans were first recognized in Europe in the eighteenth century. They had probably been brought there from China. For over a century soybeans were not used for much by Europeans, although they had long been used for food in China. Gradually, however, scientists began to understand how healthy the soybean is. Other scientists began to find more uses for the simple bean, and farmers began to discover that the soybean is easy to grow and that there are many uses for it. **6**

The major producer of soybeans in the world is the United States (see the table below), even though soybeans are not as commonly used for food in the United States as they are in other countries. In fact, Americans eat ninety-nine pounds of meat for every one pound of soy-based food. The United States exports about one third of its soybean crop. Japan is the largest importer of soybeans in the world, importing about four million tons. **7**

Country	Thousands of Tons of Soybeans Produced
United States	50,643
Brazil	15,537
China	9,710
Argentina	6,700
Canada	934
India	800
Mexico	789
Paraguay	660
Indonesia	615
Soviet Union	540

Table showing the production of soybeans in the ten leading producer nations in 1985.

When they come from the plant, soybeans contain about 18 percent of their weight in oil. Usually, the oil is removed before the beans are used for anything else. Soybean oil has many food and non-food uses. It is used as cooking oil by itself. It is also made into margarine and salad oils. The oil is also used in making paint, plastics, soap, ink, and even insecticides. Americans use over six gallons of soy oil per person per year. **8**

The remaining 82 percent of the soybean, the meal, is also used for a wide variety of food and non-food purposes. Most of the soybean meal produced in the United States is used to feed animals, especially cows. But because soybean meal consists of about 50 percent protein, contains little starch, and is easy for most people to digest, it is used in many different food products. It is added to other foods that include grains to make them healthier, especially baby foods, cereals, breads, and artificial meat. Americans and Europeans, just like the **9**

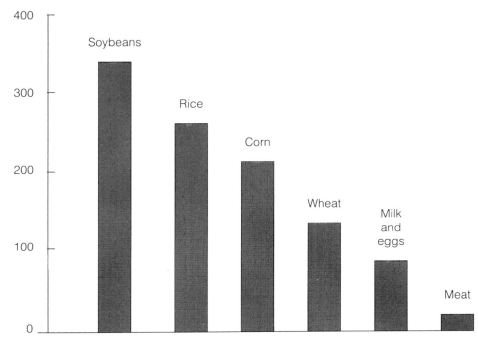

Protein (pounds)

Graph showing the amount of food protein that can be grown on one acre of land.

Chinese and Japanese before them, are also beginning to eat soybeans in the form of doufu or tofu; in baby food; as tempeh, another soy-based food that comes from Indonesia; and as soybean sprouts when the seeds are allowed to begin to grow and are eaten as green vegetables.

As the amount of land available for growing food is getting smaller, and as it becomes more important to use our available land in the most efficient way, it is becoming more important that we all begin to change our eating habits and eat more food that uses land efficiently. Of the major foods that are consumed in the modern world, soybeans are among the most efficient users of land (see the graph above). They produce more usable protein for the amount of land used than any other food, especially meat.

10

COMPREHENSION QUESTIONS

Working alone or with another student, answer the following questions about the reading. You will probably not remember the answers to all the questions. If you do not remember, look back at the reading to find the answer. For some questions, several answers may be possible. Be ready to give reasons why you think your answer is best.

1. What size are soybeans?

_____

2. What color are they?

_____

3. Where were soybeans first grown by farmers, and when?

_____

4. Why did Europeans and Americans take so long to begin to use soybeans?

_____

5. Why do you think the United States produces so many soybeans when people there do not eat many soybeans?

_____

6. How much would China have to increase its production of soybeans to equal that of the United States?

_____

7. Why do you think Japan has to import so many soybeans?

_____

8. Describe the process for making doufu.

_____

_____

_____

9. When finished, what does doufu mostly consist of?

_____

10. What part of the soybean is the most important commercial product?

_____

11. What is the most important use for soybean meal?

_____

12. Why is soybean meal often added to other foods?

_____

13. List five uses for soybean oil.

_____

_____

_____

_____

14. Why are soybeans probably going to be an important agricultural product in the future?

_____

_____

15. If we can produce one pound of protein from a piece of land by growing wheat, about how much protein can we produce from the same amount of land by growing soybeans?

_____

16. What do you think is going to happen to the cost of meat in the future? Why?

_____

_____

INFORMATION IDENTIFICATION

Read the following statements. If the information was in the reading, write *Y* before the statement. If the information was not in the reading, write *N* before the statement.

1. _____ Soybean meal is about 50 percent protein.

(Continued at top of next page)

2. _____ The salt used to make doufu comes from the sea.

3. _____ Some soybeans are gray.

4. _____ Soybean oil is used to make paint.

5. _____ Indonesians eat food made from soybeans.

6. _____ Japanese farmers grow a lot of soybeans.

7. _____ Doufu contains many vitamins.

8. _____ Americans are starting to eat more tofu.

9. _____ Machines can easily pick soybeans.

10. _____ Soybean sprouts come from Indonesia.

NEW INFORMATION

Write five pieces of information that you learned from the reading. Compare your list with the lists of two other students. How many different pieces of information did your group come up with? Which group in class had the most pieces of information?

1. _____

2. _____

3. _____

4. _____

5. _____

VOCABULARY EXERCISE

Below are some phrases that appear in the reading. Working with a partner, write definitions for each word in the phrase and then for the two words together. Compare your answers with those of other students, and write the best definitions that you hear.

Example: green vegetable
   green: _a color; the color of grass and leaves; a mixture of blue and yellow_
   vegetable: _food that comes from a plant_
   green vegetable: _food that comes from a plant and is the color of grass or leaves_

healthy food (paragraph 5)

    healthy: _____

    food: _____

    healthy food: _____

    _____

cooking oil (paragraph 8)

    cooking: _____

    oil: _____

    cooking oil: _____

    _____

salad oil (paragraph 8)

    salad: _____

    oil: _____

    salad oil: _____

    _____

soy oil (paragraph 8)

    soy: _____

    oil: _____

    soy oil: _____

    _____

baby food (paragraph 9)

    baby: _____

    food: _____

    baby food: _____

    _____

artificial meat (paragraph 9)

artificial: _____

meat: _____

artificial meat: _____

_____

OPTIONAL APPLICATION ACTIVITIES

Problem Solving

Gosnia is an imaginary country where the people are accustomed to eating a lot of beef. The population of Gosnia, however, has grown very fast, and now there are many people and not much land. Beef has become very expensive, and the poor people of Gosnia cannot afford it. The government has developed two plans, one to provide several soybean-based foods, and another to make fish available. Both foods are much cheaper than beef and are very healthy, but the people of Gosnia do not like them and have not bought them. What do you think the government of Gosnia can and should do to encourage the people to begin to eat the new foods?

Working with a group of other students, agree on at least one thing the government can do. When you are finished, share your answers with students from other groups and see how many good suggestions you have found. You might list the suggestions on the board and, in groups or as a class, rank them from best to worst.

Contest

Below are the names of four types of food. Individually, in pairs, or in small groups, list the names of as many foods of that type as you can. When your instructor tells you to stop, see who has the longest list. You will get one point for every correct answer. Take one point off for every food in the wrong column and one-half point off for every food misspelled.

MEAT	SEAFOOD	VEGETABLES	FRUIT
_____	_____	_____	_____
_____	_____	_____	_____
_____	_____	_____	_____
_____	_____	_____	_____

(Continued at top of next page)

MEAT	SEAFOOD	VEGETABLES	FRUIT
_____	_____	_____	_____
_____	_____	_____	_____
_____	_____	_____	_____
_____	_____	_____	_____
_____	_____	_____	_____
_____	_____	_____	_____
_____	_____	_____	_____
_____	_____	_____	_____

Which student had the longest list? _____

How many points did you get? _____

CHAPTER REVIEW

In this chapter you have read about nutrition, vegetarianism, the origins of some foods, and the soybean. Answer the following questions about the readings. Work alone and answer for yourself. Most of the questions do not have one correct answer; the answers are your opinion or are true for you. When you are finished, discuss your answers with your instructor and the rest of the class.

1. Which reading did you learn the most from? Why?

_____

_____

2. Write five pieces of information that you learned from reading this chapter:

a. _____

_____

b. _____

_____

(Continued at top of next page)

c. _____

_____

d. _____

_____

e. _____

_____

3. Which reading was the most interesting? Why?

_____

_____

4. Which reading was the easiest to read? Why?

_____

_____

5. Which reading was the most difficult to read? Why?

_____

_____

6. Which reading had the most personal experience or opinion in it?

_____

_____

7. Which reading had the most research in it?

_____

Now that you have read and thought about food and nutrition, write three questions that you have about the subject.

Example:
What do people who live in deserts eat, and where do they get their food?

1. _____

2. _____

3. _____

Working in groups or as a class, agree on three questions that you think are the most interesting. Then, as a group, decide where you might find the answers to these questions. You might need to look in a particular book or encyclopedia, or interview a particular person. If there is time, go as a group and find the answers to the questions.

WRITING OR SPEAKING SUMMARY

Choose one of the following topics. Then, using the information and language you have learned in this chapter, information you already have, and information you learn from other sources, write at least one page on that topic or prepare to talk to the rest of the class about it.

1. What different foods do you think your grandchildren will eat? That is, where you plan to be living, what changes in food do you think will occur over the next fifty to one hundred years? Give reasons for the changes you describe.

2. Among the conveniences that technology has made available is prepared food, food that is ready for cooking or is already cooked. Many busy people like to use prepared foods, but many others complain that prepared foods are not as good, or not as good for us, as foods prepared at home. Compare prepared food with home-cooked food. What are the advantages and disadvantages of each?

3. Many cultures and even families have beliefs about what foods can and cannot be eaten together. If you know about such a belief, describe the belief and what is thought will happen if the foods are eaten together.

4. In many families, cultures, or religions, some foods are believed to be very healthy or otherwise important. If you know about such a belief, describe the food and why and how it is important.

READING JOURNAL

List the outside reading you did while studying this chapter. (Include the title or type of material, length, topic or subject, and where you found the material.)

_____

_____

_____

Write a journal entry for this outside reading. Your instructor will want to look at your journal and may ask you to tell the rest of the class about something you read.

In your journal you might answer the following questions. Or you can write about anything else you felt or learned as you were reading.

What was the most interesting thing you read? Why was it interesting?

What was the least interesting thing you read? Why was it not interesting?

What is one piece of information you learned about food from your outside reading?

Was the reading you did difficult or easy? Why do you think it was difficult or easy?

Do you have questions about food that you can find the answers to by reading? What are they? What can you read to find the answers?

Did you enjoy the outside reading you did while you studied this chapter? Why or why not?

Chapter
5

TYING THE KNOT

RECIPE FOR A HAPPY MARRIAGE
1 cup of politeness
1 cup of flattery
2 cups of kindness
1 gallon of faith in God
a reasonable budget
a small amount of in-laws
2 teaspoons of "I am sorry"
1 cup of contentment
2 children
1 large or 2 small hobbies
1 cup of ability to ignore the other's faults
—Anonymous Folk Advice

INTRODUCTION

Although the "recipe" above is intended to be fun, it is also intended to contain some good advice. Working with a partner or in a group, try to understand what the "recipe" means. Then decide in your group if you would add anything to the advice or take anything away. See if the whole class can agree on a revised version of the "recipe."

VOCABULARY INTRODUCTION

Below are some words that are related to the subject of marriage. Work with a group of students in the class and see if you know what these words mean. If you do not know, ask other students, ask your instructor, or look in a dictionary to find out what the words mean. Write the definition of each word you did not know.

bride	fiancee	marry
ceremony	groom	spouse
couple	husband	wedding
custom	marriage	wife
family	married	

DEFINITIONS OF WORDS YOU DID NOT KNOW:

1. _____

2. _____

3. _____

4. _____

5. _____

6. _____

7. _____

8. _____

Working with other students in your group, write on the lines below ten other words that you think are related to marriage. When you are finished, you or your instructor can write the words that the class thought of on the blackboard.

_____ _____ _____

_____ _____ _____

_____ _____ _____

_____

Write on the lines below any word written on the blackboard that you are not sure you know the meaning of.

_____ _____ _____

_____ _____ _____

_____ _____ _____

Review these words as you complete this chapter.

OUTSIDE READING

Doing outside reading about marriage will help you to understand this chapter better. Popular magazines often have articles about the marriages of famous people. Other magazines are full of advice about how to have a good marriage. Libraries have books that describe marriage customs and stories or novels about marriage.

Take a few minutes in class and suggest outside readings about marriage and where to find them. Write on the lines below some good suggestions that you hear.

_____

_____

_____

_____

_____

Be sure to write about your outside reading in your Reading Journal.

INFORMATION GATHERING

Below are two groups of questions—one for married students and the other for single students. Work with another student and ask him or her all the questions that apply. Write the answers to the questions on a piece of paper. When you are finished, describe your partner's answers to the rest of the class.

For Married Students

1. How many times have you been married?
2. How old were you when you got married? How old was your spouse?
3. Who chose the person you married?
4. What was the most important thing that made you decide to marry your spouse?
5. Who had to approve of the marriage?
6. Did you have an engagement? How long was it? (An engagement is the time between when you agree to marry and when you actually get married.)
7. Who planned the wedding?
8. Who paid for the wedding?
9. Where was your wedding ceremony?
10. How did the government learn about your marriage?
11. Was there a celebration after the marriage? If there was, where was it and how many people came?
12. What property or money was exchanged between your family and your spouse's family?

13. What do you like best about being married?
14. What is the biggest difficulty or problem you have being married?

For Single Students

Do you want to get married in the future? If *yes,* answer questions 1 to 7; if *no,* answer questions 8 to 13.

1. At what age do you want to get married?
2. What is the best reason to marry someone (love, family connections, money, appearance, etc.)?
3. Do you think a wife should stay home or work outside of the home?
4. Do you want to have children? How many?
5. Who will choose your future spouse?
6. Would you marry someone from another country? Another religion?
7. Do you want to have a big wedding ceremony or a small one?

*   *   *   *   *

8. Why do you not want to get married?
9. What is the biggest problem with being married?
10. What is most enjoyable about being married?
11. Would anything make you change your mind about getting married? What?
12. Are any of your brothers or sisters married?
13. Would you like to adopt a child even though you are not planning to get married?

S H O R T   R E A D I N G

Read the following passage slowly and carefully.

Marriage Records

Most people get married only one time during their life, but some people do it again and again. In many countries men and women can divorce and remarry other people, and in some cultures it is possible for a man to marry several wives at one time. In other cultures women can marry several husbands. The laws of most countries now allow a man or a woman to have only one spouse at a time.   1

One man in the United States has been married twenty-two times, to twenty-two different women. He has been married more times than anyone else that we know about in the United States or Europe. The man, Mr. Wolf, is seventy-nine years old, and his newest wife is twenty.   2

Mr. Wolf has never remained married very long, but a couple in India has. They were married when they were five years old and have remained married to   3 each other for eighty-six years. Their marriage is the longest marriage that we know about.

QUESTIONS

1. Write any information that you learned from this passage on the lines below.

a. _____

b. _____

c. _____

2. Can you think of a subject for a fourth paragraph to the passage? Working with a partner or small group of students, write a fourth paragraph on the lines below, using your own ideas. The information you use does not have to be true. When you are finished, read your ending to the rest of the class. The class will decide which group's ending was the best.

_____

_____

_____

_____

_____

_____

FILL-IN-THE-BLANK

Working with another student, fill in the blanks in the following passage. For many of the blanks, more than one answer will be possible or correct, but put only one word in each blank. Look carefully at the sentences that come before and after the blank to be sure that the word you choose has meaning in both the sentence and the paragraph and that the form of the word is correct for that sentence. Discuss with your partner any differences in the words you choose, your understanding of the sentences, and your reasons for choosing certain words. The purpose of the exercise is to try to find as many words that can fit in the blanks as possible.

When you and your partner have finished, your instructor will ask you to compare your answers with the answers that your classmates gave. Your instructor may ask you to write your words on the blackboard. Be ready to explain why you chose a word and what the word means. Also be ready to change your answer if other students found a better word. Write other good answers that you hear below the ones that you gave.

Marriage

A marriage is the joining of a man and a woman. When a man and a woman want to live together or to _____ _____, and become husband and
                                   (1)   (2)

_____, they usually have a _____ ceremony. The man and the
    (3)   (4)

woman in a wedding are called the _____ and the _____. A man
                                  (5)   (6)

also calls the woman he is going to marry his fiancee.

Most couples in the United States go to a _____ for their wedding
                                           (7)

ceremony. The priest or the minister of the religion also makes the marriage

_____ by telling the government about the marriage. The couple usually
  (8)

exchange or give _____ to each other, and the _____ or
                (9)   (10)

_____ prays for them and their marriage. When the ceremony is over, the
  (11)

man and woman are _____ and wife, or spouses.
                      (12)

L O N G   R E A D I N G   1

PREREADING ACTIVITY

Read the title of the following story. What do you think it means? Choose one of the following:

    a. I divorced a woman and married her again.

    b. I married a woman with the same name as my first wife.

    c. I had two wedding ceremonies with the same woman.

Now read the story quickly (in about five or ten minutes) and check your guess about the title. Also try to learn the main ideas of the story, such as who it is about, what happens, and where.

I Married the Same Woman Twice

When I was young, a friend said to me, "You are going to marry outside of your culture." I did not believe him then, but when I did get married that is exactly what I did, and I did it twice. Actually, I married the same woman twice. **1**

My wife was from India, but I was born and raised in the United States. Because we came from two places that were so different and so far apart, we had to have two wedding ceremonies. One of these was in India and one of them in the United States; one for her family and one for mine. **2**

The first wedding took place in India. I had been to India before, but had never seen a wedding. As a result, my own wedding was completely strange for me. I remember that I asked my fiancee and her family many questions about the ceremony before it took place, but I did not understand much of what they told me. This was because much of what they were describing was new to me. **3**

The day of the wedding, my fiancee's brother brought her some gold jewelry and put it on her. My future mother-in-law brought out some new clothes and other gifts for me. Putting on these new clothes and jewelry was a traditional part of the wedding. **4**

The wedding ceremony began in the early evening and took place inside a square enclosure made of flowers. I wore my new clothes, and my fiancee wore a red sari and her new gold jewelry. A priest from one of the many Hindu groups in India was going to marry us. The three of us sat around a small table inside the enclosure. The table was covered with sweet things to eat and with necklaces made of flowers. Behind the priest a sign with the words "God Is Love" was hanging on the flower wall. **5**

In India it is the custom for the fathers of the bride and groom to introduce them to the priest. My fiancee's father introduced her, but since my father was not there, a friend of the family introduced me. **6**

Just before the wedding started, the priest quietly told me that I should not worry or be nervous because the ceremony would be short and mostly in English. But he was wrong. He talked for almost an hour, and he spoke mostly in Sanskrit. I did not understand very much except when he told us to put the necklaces of flowers around each other's necks and to give each other some of the sweets to eat. Then, in English, he talked about marriage. He said that it was a partnership between two people and that both people had to give something to make the marriage a good one. **7**

At the end of the ceremony all three of us put our hands together and prayed. Then we signed some papers so the government would know that the marriage was legal, and we were married. **8**

Two weeks later we were back in the United States and we had to have another ceremony. We had this ceremony so my family could see us get married. The ceremony in the United States was in a small Lutheran church in my hometown. I was very familiar with this kind of ceremony because I had seen it many times and had even been part of some ceremonies as an attendant. In the United **9**

States, the bride's father usually brings her to the front of the church where the groom and minister are waiting. My bride's father was not there, but a friend of her family was there, so he brought her to the front of the church. We both dressed in our best clothes. I wore the suit I had worn in India, and my wife wore a new white sari that she had brought with her.

Because we were already legally married, this ceremony was only a religious **10** one. Also, it was all in English. We stood in front of the minister at the front of the church. He told us about our responsibilities as a married couple, asked us to promise to try to have a good marriage, and then prayed for us and for our marriage. Usually people in the United States give each other wedding rings at this part of the ceremony, but we did not like to wear rings, so we did not exchange them. We knew the ceremony was over when the minister told us that we could kiss each other.

Not many people get married twice to the same person. I have heard of **11** couples who have a kind of wedding ceremony every year, and I have heard of couples who have a wedding again after twenty-five or fifty years of marriage. Of course, I did not really get married twice. Only the first ceremony was a legal or official one. I did have two weddings, though. If you are married, you can probably guess how difficult two weddings can be. Or how much fun. But if you are not married, take my advice. Do it only once!

QUESTIONS

1. Look again at your guess about what the title means. What do you think of your answer now? Do you want to leave it the same, or do you want to change it? What did other students guess?

2. Who is the story about? _____

_____

3. What happens in the story? _____

_____

4. Where does the story take place? _____

_____

COMPLETION

Now read the story again. Then, working with a partner or in a group, complete the following sentences with information from the story. Try not to use the exact words that were in the story. Sometimes more than one answer will be possible.

1. The couple's first ceremony _____

_____

2. The bride's family was not _____

_____

3. The groom did not understand the Indian ceremony because _____

_____

4. Only one of the marriage ceremonies _____

_____

5. In the United States, the wedding ceremony _____

_____

6. The bride wore _____

_____

7. The couple was legally married when _____

_____

8. The man knew about weddings in the United States because _____

_____

9. The writer's advice is _____

_____

INFORMATION IDENTIFICATION

Read the statements below and at the top of the next page. If the statement is true about the Indian ceremony, write *I* in the blank. If it is true about the ceremony in the United States, write *US* in the blank. If the statement is true about both, write *B*. If it is not true about either, write *N*.

1. _____ The bride wore a red sari.

2. _____ The bride and groom exchanged rings.

3. _____ The bride and groom exchanged necklaces of flowers and sweets.

4. _____ The groom was familiar with this ceremony.

5. _____ The bride's father gave her gold jewelry.

6. _____ The ceremony was unofficial.

7. _____ A friend of the bride's family brought her to the wedding.

8. _____ The ceremony took place inside a church.

9. _____ The wedding ceremony was religious.

10. _____ The bride's mother brought gifts for the groom.

COMPARISON

Complete the following lists. When you have finished, your instructor or one of the students in the class will write on the blackboard all the different answers written by students in the class. Compare your answers with those written by other students. Did you write the same answers or did you write different ones?

1. List three differences between the ceremony in India and the ceremony in the United States.

_____

_____

_____

2. List three similarities between the two ceremonies.

_____

_____

_____

VOCABULARY EXERCISE

On the next page, circle the best definition of the words from the reading.

1. In paragraph 4 you read the phrase *my future mother-in-law*. The best meaning for this phrase is:

    a. the woman I am going to marry

    b. a woman who is going to be a mother

    c. the mother of the woman I am going to marry

2. In paragraph 5 you read the word *enclosure*. The best meaning for *enclosure* in that paragraph is:

    a. something made of clothing

    b. a place for clothing

    c. an area surrounded by a fence or wall

3. In paragraphs 5 and 7 you read the word *necklaces*. The best meaning for *necklace* in those paragraphs is:

    a. something worn around the neck

    b. jewelry

    c. a kind of cloth

4. In paragraph 7 you read the word *worry*. The best meaning for *worry* in that paragraph is:

    a. feel happy and excited

    b. feel sad or unhappy

    c. feel nervous or a little afraid

5. In paragraph 8 you read the word *legal,* and in paragraph 10 you read the phrase *legally married.* The best meaning for *legal* in those paragraphs is:

    a. accepted or approved by the government

    b. permanent

    c. done by a religious person

6. In paragraph 9 you read the word *hometown*. The best meaning of *hometown* in that paragraph is:

    a. poor or small town or city

    b. place someone is living now

    c. city or town someone originally comes from

L O N G   R E A D I N G   2

PREREADING ACTIVITY

The following reading is about marriage between people from different countries. Before you read, think about what you know about this subject. Do you know any married couples in which the partners come from different countries? Working in groups, make a list of the countries the partners in the international marriages you know come from. When all the groups are done, the instructor will find out how many countries each group listed.

COUNTRIES		COUNTRIES	
One spouse /	Other spouse	One spouse /	Other spouse
_____	_____	_____	_____
_____	_____	_____	_____
_____	_____	_____	_____
_____	_____	_____	_____
_____	_____	_____	_____
_____	_____	_____	_____
_____	_____	_____	_____
_____	_____	_____	_____

Marriages sometimes have problems, and international marriages have their own kinds of problems. Working with a group of other students, list five problems that you think might occur in international marriages.

1. _____

2. _____

3. _____

4. _____

5. _____

Now read the following selection and see if the problems Masako and Ahmed had were similar to the problems on your list. Read slowly and carefully, taking about twenty to thirty minutes.

Marriage International

As travel and communication become easier, and as more and more people   1
live, work, and study far away from their home countries, the more marriage between partners from different countries and cultures increases. While increasingly common, such marriages can bring problems as well as happiness and satisfaction.

Among the problems that those involved in international marriages encounter   2
are problems of loneliness, miscommunication, differences in expectations, and the loss of family and cultural support.

One partner in an international marriage can experience these feelings if and   3
when the couple move or stay away from that partner's home country and culture. The wife or husband is separated from her or his family, friends, and familiar surroundings and must develop new friends and ways of behaving. When the couple is first married, problems like this may seem unimportant. The partners are sure that they will be happy with each other and that problems of loneliness and separation will be taken care of by their partner. As the marriage matures, however, and it becomes clearer that the husband or wife "cannot be all things" to the other, loneliness and separation sometimes turn into serious problems. The lonely partner may want to return to the familiar surroundings of home, country, and family and may resent the partner's happiness. Unless some understanding or solution is reached, this loneliness may lead to greater and greater problems between the spouses.

Masako is from Japan, and her husband, Ahmed, is from Morocco. Masako   4
and Ahmed were married when they were both students in the United States. Before they married, they visited Japan and Morocco and hoped that they would continue to visit both countries after their marriage. Ahmed and Masako stayed in the United States for four years after they were married while they studied for their Ph.D. degrees. After four years, Ahmed's father became ill, and his family asked him to return to Morocco to take care of the family's business. Masako and Ahmed went to Morocco and have been living there for the last five years.

At first, Masako liked Morocco. It was new and exciting and exotic. The food   5
was good and the people were friendly, although both were different from what she had known in Japan. Ahmed's family was also very good to her.

After a year or so, however, Masako began to miss her family and friends and   6
to dislike much of what she saw in Morocco. Ahmed was busy with his business, but Masako was not able to find a job. She helped Ahmed in the business, but the family did not want her to work too hard so they made sure she spent a lot of time

with Ahmed's mother and sisters. The couple did not have time to travel back to Japan.

Masako could not cook Japanese food in Morocco because she could not   7
find many of the ingredients and because the couple usually ate with Ahmed's family, who did not like Japanese food. She also did not like the weather in Morocco, where it was hot and dry much of the time, and wished she could feel the cool, humid air of Japan. Morocco seemed brown and harsh to her.

Most importantly, Masako had few friends in Morocco and no one she could   8
really talk to about her feelings. Few members of Ahmed's family spoke English and none spoke Japanese, and Masako spoke no Arabic or French.

Masako tried to talk about her feelings to Ahmed. At first he was sympathetic   9
and tried to understand and help, but as Masako's loneliness grew stronger, he became less able to understand how she was feeling. He was busy in his business and with his mother and brothers and sisters.

After two years in Morocco, Masako went to Ahmed and told him that she   10
wanted to go back to Japan to see her family and maybe to get a job. She did not want to divorce Ahmed, but she wanted to spend some time with her family and to find out whether she wanted to spend the rest of her life in Morocco or not.

Ahmed was very upset when he heard that Masako wanted to return to Japan.   11
He was afraid that his family would be angry with him, but he was even more afraid that he was going to lose Masako, whom he loved very much. At first he told Masako that she could not go back to Japan and that he did not want to talk about it anymore. But after a couple of weeks of seeing how unhappy Masako had become, he realized that something had to be done. Talking with Masako had become very difficult because she was so unhappy that she cried much of the time. Although he was afraid of what she would say, Ahmed finally talked to his mother about the problem. Instead of being angry with him, Ahmed's mother was very understanding and very helpful. She gave Ahmed some excellent advice.

Masako and Ahmed are now happy with their marriage.   12

DID YOU THINK OF IT?

Make a list of the problems that Masako and Ahmed had. After each one, write down whether it was a problem that you thought of before you read the selection.

Problem	*Did you think of it?*
1. _____	_____
2. _____	_____
3. _____	_____

4. _____ _____

5. _____ _____

6. _____ _____

7. _____ _____

8. _____ _____

GIVING ADVICE

Working in groups, describe what you think Ahmed's mother's advice was and what the couple did to work out the problems in their marriage. Be specific. What exactly did Ahmed's mother tell him? What did the couple do first? What did they do about Masako's loneliness? What are they doing now to keep the problem from returning?

When your group has finished, share your description with the rest of the class. After you have heard the other groups' advice, work together as a class and write an ending to the story.

INFORMATION IDENTIFICATION

Below are some statements about international marriage. If the information was in the reading, write *Y* before the statement. If the information was not in the reading, write *N* before the statement.

Example:

____N____ **International marriages increased by 14 percent last year.**

1. _____ International marriages can bring happiness as well as problems.

2. _____ Most international couples live in the home country of one of the spouses.

3. _____ Partners in international marriages usually discuss their problems before they get married.

4. _____ Ahmed and Masako were both graduate students.

5. _____ Masako enjoyed living in Morocco for about a year.

(Continued at top of next page)

6. _____ Masako and Ahmed had anticipated their difficulties in living in Morocco.

7. _____ Ahmed's family's business was not doing well, and the business had Ahmed worried.

8. _____ Masako had many old friends in Japan.

9. _____ Ahmed called a meeting of his family to discuss what he and Masako should do.

10. _____ Ahmed was afraid to talk to his mother about the problems he and Masako were having.

VOCABULARY EXERCISE

1. In paragraph 1 there is a phrase that means "country where someone is from." Write that phrase here:

_____

2. In paragraph 3 there is a phrase that means "to take care of everything someone needs." Write that phrase here:

_____

3. In paragraph 3 there is a word that means "to feel bad toward someone because of what they have or what they have done." Write that word here:

_____.

4. In paragraph 5 there is a word that means "strange, foreign, different." Write that word here: _____.

5. In paragraph 7 there is a word that means "full of moisture or water." Write that word here: _____.

6. In paragraph 9 there is a word that means "having similar feelings." Write that word here: _____.

L O N G   R E A D I N G   3

PREREADING ACTIVITY

In this reading you will learn more about marriage customs. Look over the reading quickly (in five or ten minutes) to find the answers to the following questions:

1. How many customs does the writer describe?
2. What are those customs?
3. What does the writer try to find out about each custom?

Rice, Rings, and Rituals

Weddings are a kind of ritual. That is, they are ceremonies, full of customs and traditions, performed the same way by almost everyone who is a member of that community or culture. People sometimes know the reasons for customs or how they started, but, more often, we do what the custom requires us to do without knowing why or how the custom began.   1

When we do not know the source or origin of a custom, it is interesting to try to find out how it started or even to guess at what it means.   2

One custom that is common at weddings in the United States is throwing rice at the bride and groom as they leave the place where the wedding ceremony was held. No one knows exactly why people throw rice. Although at some weddings the well-wishers now throw birdseed, it would be very strange or funny to most of us if someone threw beans or some other vegetable. One explanation for the throwing of rice is that the rice is supposed to make certain that the couple will have many children. If this is true, then the custom is not always a good one now because many couples do not want a lot of children. Another explanation for the rice-throwing custom is that the rice was there to keep the gods or spirits satisfied so they would bring good luck to the couple. Actually, we do not really know how or why the custom of throwing rice at weddings began.   3

In many wedding ceremonies the bride and groom have attendants, other men and women who are part of the wedding ceremony but who do not have any official purpose for being there. Their presence is a custom. The reason for the custom may be that many centuries ago, ten witnesses were required to make a wedding official. Now, we still have the attendants although they are not officially required.   4

One more common custom is making some kind of loud noise after the wedding with bells, horns, or even tin cans tied to the couple's car. This custom is certainly fun for everyone, and it tells the rest of the world that a wedding has taken place. Some people believe that the purpose of the noise, like the purpose   5 of throwing rice, was to keep bad luck away. Maybe that is true and maybe not, but the custom is still an enjoyable one. That is enough reason to keep the custom alive.

QUESTIONS

Now write the answers you found for the questions at the beginning of the reading.

1. How many customs does the writer describe?

_____

2. What are those customs?

_____

3. What does the writer try to find out about each custom?

_____

Does everyone in the class agree on the answers?

COMPLETION

Summarize the main ideas of the reading by completing the following sentences. Work with a partner if your instructor asks you to.

1. One custom found at weddings is _____

_____

_____ .

2. It is possible that one reason for throwing rice is _____

_____

_____ , but we really do not know _____ .

3. Another custom is for the bride and groom to have _____ .

4. A third custom is for people at the wedding to make _____ .

PARAPHRASE

Below are five sentences from the reading. After each sentence are two other sentences, one of which has about the same meaning as the sentence from the reading. Put a check (√) before the sentence that has the same meaning.

Example:

Actually, we do not really know how or why the custom of throwing rice at weddings began.

    a. _____ The custom of throwing rice actually began at weddings.

    b. _√_ The origin or beginning of the custom of throwing rice is unknown.

1. When we do not know the source or origin of a custom, it is interesting to try to find out how it started or even to guess at what it means.

    a. _____ It is interesting to try to learn how customs began.

    b. _____ We must find the origin of interesting customs.

2. Although at some weddings the well-wishers now throw birdseed, it would be very strange or funny to most of us if someone threw beans or some other vegetable.

    a. _____ Throwing beans or other vegetables would be as funny as throwing birdseed.

    b. _____ Throwing beans or other vegetables at weddings would be funny, but throwing birdseed is not.

3. If this is true, then the custom is not always a good one now because many couples do not want a lot of children.

    a. _____ The custom has stopped because couples do want to have children.

    b. _____ Because couples do not want to have children, the custom does not have a good reason.

4. Now, we still have the attendants although they are not officially required.

    a. _____ Attendants are still in weddings but they are not necessary to make the wedding official.

    b. _____ Officially, attendants cannot be in wedding ceremonies.

(Continued at top of next page)

5. Some people believe that the purpose of the noise, like the purpose of throwing rice, was to keep bad luck away.

    a. _____ It is possible that the purpose of making noise and throwing rice was to keep bad luck away.

    b. _____ Some people believe that throwing rice and making noise had different purposes.

GUESSING

By yourself, or in small groups, try to guess the reasons for the following marriage customs or how they started. When you are finished, tell the other students in the class what your guesses are. As a class, decide which guesses are the best.

1. The bride wears a veil—a thin cloth that covers her face—just before and during the ceremony. She takes it off at the end of the ceremony.

_____

_____

_____

2. The groom should not see the bride on the wedding day, especially if she is wearing her wedding dress.

_____

_____

_____

3. The bride throws her bouquet of flowers to a group of unmarried female friends at the wedding.

_____

_____

_____

VOCABULARY EXERCISE

Circle the best answer.

1. In the title and in paragraph 1 you read the word _ritual_. The best meaning for _ritual_ is:

    a. something done in the right way

    b. a ceremony usually performed in a similar way every time

    c. a kind of wedding

2. In paragraph 3 you read the word _well-wisher_. The best meaning for _well-wisher_ is:

    a. someone who wants someone else to be happy

    b. someone who wishes by a well

    c. someone who does a good job wishing

3. In paragraph 3 you read the word *birdseed*. The best meaning for *birdseed* in that paragraph is:

    a. seed made from birds

    b. seed for birds to eat

    c. seed that birds grow from

4. In paragraph 4 you read the word *witnesses*. The best meaning for *witnesses* in that paragraph is:

    a. people who see a wedding happen

    b. priests who perform a marriage ceremony

    c. people who stay in an office

5. In paragraph 4 you read the word *officially*. The best meaning for *officially* in that paragraph is:

    a. accepted or approved by the government

    b. permanent

    c. done in an office

CROSSWORD PUZZLE

Fill in the crossword puzzle below with words related to marriage.

ACROSS

2. A wedding _____ is often made of gold.
6. Sometimes people throw this at weddings.
7. A wife gets one of these.
8. Unfortunately, marriages sometimes end in _____.
9. Many guests often attend the wedding _____.
10. A husband or a wife is a _____.

DOWN

1. The woman getting married.
3. A husband and wife are called a _____.
4. When two people get married, they usually have a _____.
5. The man getting married.
9. A tradition or old way of doing something.

CHAPTER REVIEW

In this chapter you have read about marriage records, a man who got married twice, international marriages, and marriage customs. Answer the following questions about the readings. Work alone and answer for yourself. Most of the questions do not have one correct answer; the answers are your opinion or are true for you. When you are finished, discuss your answers with your instructor and the rest of the class.

1. Which reading did you learn the most from? Why?

_____

_____

2. Write five pieces of information that you learned from reading this chapter:

a. _____

_____

b. _____

_____

c. _____

_____

d. _____

_____

e. _____

_____

3. Which reading was the most interesting? Why?

_____

_____

4. Which reading was the easiest to read? Why?

_____

_____

5. Which reading was the most difficult to read? Why?

_____

_____

6. Which reading had the most personal experience or opinion in it?

_____

7. Which reading had the most research in it?

_____

Now that you have read and thought about marriage, write three questions that you still have about the topic.

Example:
At what age do people usually get married in China? _____

1. _____

2. _____

3. _____

Working in groups or as a class, agree on three questions that you think are the most interesting. Then, as a group, try to decide where you might find the answers to these questions. You might need to look in a particular book or encyclopedia, or interview a particular person. If there is time, go as a group to find the answers to the questions.

WRITING OR SPEAKING SUMMARY

Choose one of the following topics. Then write at least a page on the subject or prepare to talk about it for five or ten minutes. Give your talk or read your paper to the rest of the class, and be ready to answer questions about it.

1. Describe a wedding, your own or another you know well. Explain why it was memorable or special.
2. Compare marriage fifty or one hundred years ago with marriage today in a country or culture you know well. What was better or easier in the past, and what is better or easier now? What was worse or harder in the past, and what is worse or harder now?
3. How do you think marriage will change in the next one hundred years? (You might want to specify what country or culture you are describing.)

READING JOURNAL

List the outside reading you did while studying this chapter. (Include the title or type of material, length, topic or subject, and where you found the material.)

_____

_____

_____

Write a journal entry for this outside reading. Your instructor will want to look at your journal and may ask you to tell the rest of the class about something you read. In your journal you might answer the following questions. Or you can write about anything else you felt or learned as you were reading.

What was the most interesting thing you read? Why was it interesting?

What was the least interesting thing you read? Why was it not interesting?

What is one piece of information you learned about marriage from your outside reading?

Was the reading you did difficult or easy? Why do you think it was difficult or easy?

Do you have questions about marriage that you can find the answers to by reading? What are they? What can you read to find the answers?

Did you enjoy the outside reading you did while you studied this chapter? Why or why not?

Chapter
6
ANIMALS AND US

The lion and the lamb will lay together.
—"Lion and Lamb"
Mary Rice Hopkins

INTRODUCTION

The sentence at the top of this page comes from a song written in English. Working with another student, decide what the sentence means. What does it assume about lions and lambs? What do the lion and the lamb represent? What hope does the sentence have about the future? You may need to ask your instructor or another English speaker for help.

When you have decided on a meaning, discuss it with the students in your group to see if you all agree with the hope expressed in the sentence.

VOCABULARY INTRODUCTION

Below are some words that are related to the subject of animals. Work with a group of students in the class and see if you know what the words mean. If you do not know, ask other students, ask your instructor, or look in a dictionary to find out what the words mean. Write the definition of each word you did not know.

bird	feed	raise
cat	fish	tame
cow	monkey	train
dog	pet	wild
farm	pig	

DEFINITIONS OF WORDS YOU DID NOT KNOW:

1. _____

2. _____

3. _____

4. _____

5. _____

6. _____

7. _____

8. _____

Working with the other students in your group, write on the lines below ten other words that are related to animals. When you are finished, you or your teacher can write the words that the class thought of on the blackboard.

_____   _____   _____

_____   _____   _____

_____   _____   _____

_____

Write on the lines below any word written on the blackboard that you are not sure you know the meaning of.

_____   _____   _____

_____   _____   _____

_____   _____   _____

Review these words as you complete this chapter.

Next, think of as many animal names in English as you can and write them in the space provided. Some animal names are given at the top of each column to help you get started. The names that you write do not need to be related to these animals. Write for five minutes. When everyone has finished, students in the class will read their lists. Write the names of any animals you hear that you did not include on your list.

Cat	Dog	Horse	Snake	Fish	Bird
_____	_____	_____	_____	_____	_____
_____	_____	_____	_____	_____	_____
_____	_____	_____	_____	_____	_____
_____	_____	_____	_____	_____	_____
_____	_____	_____	_____	_____	_____
_____	_____	_____	_____	_____	_____
_____	_____	_____	_____	_____	_____
_____	_____	_____	_____	_____	_____
_____	_____	_____	_____	_____	_____
_____	_____	_____	_____	_____	_____
_____	_____	_____	_____	_____	_____
_____	_____	_____	_____	_____	_____
_____	_____	_____	_____	_____	_____
_____	_____	_____	_____	_____	_____
_____	_____	_____	_____	_____	_____

OUTSIDE READING

Doing outside reading about animals will help you to understand this chapter better. Encyclopedias are good sources of basic information about animal life and animals in different countries. Many magazines have articles about animals that are in danger of disappearing. Libraries are full of information about animals.

Take a few minutes in class and suggest outside readings about animals and where to find them. Write on the lines below some good suggestions that you hear.

_____

_____

_____

_____

_____

Be sure to write about your outside reading in your Reading Journal.

INFORMATION FOCUSING

Humans use animals in many ways—for food, for clothing, for companionship, and for work. With a partner, list the five animals that are most useful to humans. Give a reason why each animal is useful. When you are finished, compare your list with the lists of other students. Try to get the whole class to agree on one list of five animals.

YOUR LIST

Animal	Why Useful
1. _____	_____
2. _____	_____
3. _____	_____
4. _____	_____
5. _____	_____

CLASS LIST

Animal	Why Useful
1. _____	_____

2. _____   _____

3. _____   _____

4. _____   _____

5. _____   _____

S H O R T   R E A D I N G

The following reading is about farmers in the United States and the animals they raise. Scan the passage quickly, looking only for the answers to these questions:

1. What animals do farmers in the United States usually raise?
2. What kinds of animals are some farmers starting to raise?
3. Why are the farmers raising these new animals?
4. For what purpose are the farmers raising each of the following: llamas, ostriches, zebras, miniature pigs?

Exotic Animals and American Farms

In North America, more and more farmers are finding it profitable to raise animals that are not usually found on farms. In addition to the traditional cows, chickens, horses, sheep, and goats (with maybe some ducks, turkeys, and geese added in), farmers are starting to find fun and profit in raising llamas, ostriches, zebras, and miniature pigs.   **1**

The animals are raised for different purposes. Llamas, the camel-like animals from the mountains of South America, are used to carry heavy loads in the mountains of western North America. Government workers and sportsmen use llamas to carry equipment and supplies. Each llama can carry over one hundred pounds, causes little damage to the land, and needs very little water and food.   **2**

Ostriches, the large flightless birds from Africa, and zebras, the striped horse-like animals also from Africa, are raised for their skins. Since it is difficult to get good skins from wild animals in Africa because of the expense and the need to protect the few remaining animals, it is cheaper and easier to raise the animals in North America.   **3**

Miniature pigs, about the size of a medium-sized dog, are kept by some people as pets. It may be hard to believe, but the pigs can be trained and are friendly and well-behaved. They are also expensive; a miniature pig can be sold for as much as $2,000.   **4**

Farmers are learning to raise and profit from animals that previously were found only in zoos.   **5**

QUESTIONS

Now write your answers to the questions from the beginning of the reading.

1. What animals do farmers in the United States usually raise?

_____

2. What kinds of animals are some farmers starting to raise?

_____

3. Why are the farmers raising these new animals?

_____

4. For what purpose are the farmers raising each of the following:

llamas _____

ostriches _____

zebras _____

miniature pigs _____

FILL-IN-THE-BLANK

Working with another student, fill in the blanks in the following passage. For many of the blanks, more than one answer will be possible or correct, but put only one word in each blank. Look carefully at the sentences that come before and after the blank to be sure that the word you choose has meaning in both the sentence and the paragraph and that the form of the word is correct for that sentence. Discuss with your partner any differences in the words you choose, your understanding of the sentences, and your reasons for choosing certain words. The purpose of the exercise is to try to find as many words that can fit in the blanks as possible.

When you and your partner have finished, your instructor will ask you to compare your answers with the answers that your classmates gave. Your instructor may ask you to write your words on the blackboard. Be ready to explain why you chose a word and what the word means. Also be ready to change your answer if other students found a better word. Write other good answers that you hear below the ones that you gave.

Humans and Animals

Humans use animals in many ways. We use them for food, for clothing, for

transportation, and for recreation and enjoyment. Cows, sheep, pigs, chickens, and

fish are some of the animals that we commonly _____. Eggs come from
                                                          (1)

_____ and milk from _____.
        (2)   (3)

Animals also provide us with materials for clothing. Wool comes from

_____ , and leather shoes are made from animal _____.
        (4)   (5)

We _____ on horses and other large animals, and sometimes these
          (6)

animals _____ wagons full of loads that are too heavy for us to carry. Pets
              (7)

are animals that we keep around our houses for _____.
                                                          (8)

Blind people use _____ to help them walk. Dogs are also used to help
                          (9)

us _____ for other animals and for protection.
        (10)

Medical and other _____ researchers also use animals, especially
                            (11)

_____ and various kinds of monkeys.
        (12)

L O N G   R E A D I N G   1

PREREADING ACTIVITY

Can you answer these questions?

What is the largest fish in the world?

_____

What fish or what kind of fish is the most dangerous to humans?

_____

   The answer to the first question is a fact. The whale shark is the largest fish in the world. The whale shark is a kind of shark, but it is not dangerous to humans. (Remember, the whale is not a fish; it is a mammal, like elephants, horses, and dogs.)
   The second question is more difficult to answer. Few fish attack humans, and those that do attack humans do so very rarely. Most people believe that sharks are dangerous, and in some cases they are. There are over 250 kinds of sharks, and most of them, such as the whale shark and the basking shark, are completely harmless to

humans. A few species, however, such as the tiger, blue, mako, and great white shark do occasionally attack people and hurt or kill them. So the best answer to the second question may be the shark, but we really do not have many facts to support that conclusion.

The following reading is a magazine article about the great white shark, the shark that most people are afraid of.

Before you read, look at the title, and answer the following questions:

From the title, what do you think is the writer's attitude toward great white sharks?

_____

_____

_____

What words make you think that?

_____

Now read the following questions and answer any that you can. Then read the article carefully and slowly, taking about twenty minutes.

1. Generally, are most people afraid of great white sharks?

_____

2. Do great white sharks regularly attack humans?

_____

3. Where are great white sharks usually found?

_____

4. How large do great white sharks usually grow?

_____

5. What enemies do the sharks have?

_____

6. Do sharks usually kill the people they do attack?

_____

The Myth of the Monster

In January 1989, the body of a young woman was found in the ocean off of **1** California. The body was badly bitten, and biologists concluded that the woman had been killed by a great white shark.

Stories of people being killed by sharks are common, and such stories **2** strengthen the fear that many humans have of sharks. The shark that is feared the most is the great white shark, often viewed as a monster fish, a terror of the deep.

Without a doubt, the great white shark can be extremely dangerous to people. **3** But, say scientists who study the animal, our fears of it are far out of proportion to the actual danger of the animal. Despite the great white's reputation, it only occasionally attacks people and rarely kills them. "More people lose their lives to bee stings," said Bob Lea, Director of California's Department of Fish and Game.

Since 1926, there have been only sixty-eight reported shark attacks on **4** people off the West Coast of the United States, mostly by great white sharks. Approximately 90 percent of those attacks have resulted in injuries, but only seven have been fatal. On the East Coast swimmers constantly ask about the danger of attacks by great white sharks even though there have been no white shark attacks there in twenty-five years. Just the thought of the great white shark causes fear, however. "No one wants to get eaten alive," says East Coast biologist Harold Pratt.

Such fears are based on myths about great white sharks, myths that result **5** from a lack of understanding. Although widely feared, the great white shark is scientifically probably the least understood of all sharks. As one California shark expert said, "The scariest thing about great white sharks is our own ignorance of them."

The great white's size, speed, and strength have prevented scientists from **6** studying it for any length of time either in the oceans or in aquariums. "We know more about the goldfish than we do about the great white shark," says John McCosker, the director of an aquarium in San Francisco.

The great white shark can be found in many of the world's oceans, but it is **7** most commonly found along the coasts of North America, South Africa, and South Australia. Because the great white is a solitary animal, it is difficult to estimate the size of its population. Scientists think, however, that the shark's numbers are quite small.

Great white sharks have no real enemies; nothing eats the great white. The **8** largest great white shark on record was caught in 1984 off Western Australia. It was 19.5 feet long. Some biologists believe these fish may reach lengths of up to twenty-five feet and live twenty years or longer.

Little is known about the reproductive process of great white sharks, but **9** scientists think that young sharks are about 3.5 feet long at birth and are perfectly capable of catching and eating fish. Young sharks live mostly on fish until they reach lengths of nine to twelve feet, when they turn to larger mammals.

Sharks seem to have two personalities, one for hunting and eating and one for   **10**
the rest of the time. When they are not hunting and eating, great white sharks
swim calmly and show little interest in other animals around them. When hunting,
however, the great white hides in rocks on the bottom of the ocean and attacks
from below. Great whites usually attack with one quick bite to disable their victim
and then return to eat. Eating is usually done in very large bites.

Great whites sense their prey with sensors located in the front tip of their   **11**
bodies. The shark's body is designed to move through the water very quickly, and
it is only when it is ready to bite that the mouth opens and exposes the shark's
multiple rows of sharp teeth.

But even with its sharp teeth and dangerous appearance, shark attacks on   **12**
people are extremely rare, and 80 percent of shark attacks are not fatal. Scientists
believe that sharks attack people by mistake; the sharks think they are attacking
a seal or other aquatic animal. "You are probably at much greater risk driving your
car to the beach," says Bob Lea.

As knowledge about great white sharks increases and as the animal is better   **13**
understood, the myth of the shark as a monster may disappear. Even now there
are many people who would rather see the great white shark in its ocean home
than to see it killed.

(Adapted from "The Myth of the Monster" by Michael Tennesen. *National Wildlife*, Oct./Nov. 1989.)

QUESTIONS

Now write your answers to the questions from the beginning of the reading. Did
you find answers to the questions you could not answer before? Have any of your
answers changed?

1. Generally, are most people afraid of great white sharks?

_____

2. Do great white sharks regularly attack humans?

_____

3. Where are great white sharks usually found?

_____

4. How large do great white sharks usually grow?

_____

5. What enemies do the sharks have?

_____

6. Do sharks usually kill the people they do attack?

_____

COMPLETION

Working with a partner, complete the following sentences with information from the article. Do not look back at the article until you have finished. Then check your answers to see if your completions are correct.

1. The woman described at the beginning of the story had _____

_____.

2. The shark that is feared the most is _____

_____.

3. Despite the great white's reputation, it only occasionally _____

_____.

4. Most shark attacks cause injuries, but _____

_____.

5. The great white shark's size, speed, and strength make it _____

_____.

6. Scientists think that the number of great white sharks is _____

_____.

7. When great white sharks reach a length of nine to twelve feet, they _____

_____.

8. Great white sharks seem to have two personalities, _____

and _____.

9. Most shark attacks on people _____.

10. Many people would rather see great white sharks _____

_____.

NEW INFORMATION

Write five pieces of information that you learned from reading about great white sharks.

1. _____

2. _____

3. _____

4. _____

5. _____

Compare your list with those of other students. Then revise your list if any of your information is wrong or if you are reminded of more interesting or important information.

INTERVIEW

Almost everyone is afraid of some kind of animal. Interview another student in your class. Find out what animal that student is afraid of and why. Then report on your interview to the rest of the class. Make sure that the rest of the students know what the animal is. Ask other students for advice on how your partner can become less afraid of that animal.

VOCABULARY EXERCISE

Circle the best answer.

1. In paragraph 2 you read the phrase *monster fish*. The best meaning for *monster fish* in that paragraph is:

    a. large fish

    b. dangerous fish

    c. large and frightening fish

2. In paragraph 3 you read the phrase *far out of proportion*. The best meaning for this phrase is:

    a. greater than necessary

    b. caused by

    c. much less than

3. In paragraph 4 you read the word *fatal*. The best meaning for *fatal* in that paragraph is:

    a. unnecessary

    b. caused death

    c. serious

4. In paragraph 9 you read the phrase *reproductive process*. The best meaning for *reproductive process* in that paragraph is:

    a. process of growing

    b. process of eating

    c. process of producing babies or offspring

5. In paragraph 9 you read the phrase *turn to*. The best meaning for *turn to* in that paragraph is:

    a. begin to eat

    b. change into or become

    c. change direction toward

6. In paragraph 10 you read the word *disable*. The best meaning for *disable* in that paragraph is:

    a. kill

    b. cut into two pieces

    c. make helpless

7. In paragraph 11 you read the word *exposes*. The best meaning for *exposes* in that paragraph is:

    a. bites, chews

    b. discovers, finds

    c. makes visible, uncovers

8. In paragraph 12 you read the word *risk*. The best meaning for *risk* in that paragraph is:

    a. danger or chance of being hurt

    b. wanting to do something dangerous

    c. lucky

LONG READING 2

PREREADING ACTIVITY

The next reading is a newspaper article about a famous circus animal trainer, Gunther Gebel-Williams. Before you read, review what you remember about a circus that you may have seen.

Your instructor will ask you to suggest information that you might include in a description of this circus. Here are some suggestions:

How old were you when you saw the circus?

Where was the circus?

What animals did you see?

List other kinds of information you might include:

_____

_____

_____

_____

_____

Write your description of the circus on the lines below:

_____

_____

_____

_____

_____

_____

_____

_____

Now scan the article, looking only for answers to the following questions:

1. Why is this an important time for Gunther Gebel-Williams?
2. Why is Gebel-Williams important to the circus?
3. What was Gebel-Williams's special trick with animals? Which animals?
4. Will someone continue Gebel-Williams's work after he stops working for the circus?
5. What does Gebel-Williams think is most important in training animals?

The Greatest Trainer on Earth!

The door of his bus opens and out jumps Gunther Gebel-Williams, springing   1
down the steps as lightly as the tigers he's trained for the Ringling Bros. and
Barnum and Bailey Circus for four decades.

"Come, come," he says, walking quickly to the place where the elephants,   2
tigers, bears, horses, ponies, camels, llamas, and Russian wolfhounds are held
between performances. He grabs a couple of bales of hay and tosses them on the
cement.

"Now," he says, sitting on a bale and in his pinstriped suit, tie, and crisp   3
trousers looking more like a corporate executive than a wild animal trainer, "we
will talk."

This is the first time in years that Gebel-Williams, fifty-five and lithe as an   4
acrobat, has talked to the media. It might be the last. After a lifetime of performing
for circuses here and abroad, Gebel-Williams is retiring in 1990, though he hints
he may be back for special performances. He is the circus's most popular act.

Forty-five minutes of the circus's two-hour performance are devoted to   5
Gebel-Williams and the horses, tigers, and elephants he has trained. The circus
finale is an extravagant Gunther Gebel-Williams tribute that is very different from
the European circus where he got his start in 1946.

His mother had accepted a job as a seamstress for Germany's Circus   6
Williams, bringing the twelve-year-old Gunther with her. The constant traveling
made his mother quit, but Gunther stayed and was adopted by the Williams
family, whose name he eventually added to his own name. Harry Williams, an
expert horse trainer, taught young Gunther how to work with horses, and soon he
was stunt riding.

When he'd mastered horses, he worked with elephants, whose intelligence he   7
found superior. Tigers joined the act later, when Gebel-Williams "got the idea to
have a tiger in a cage with two elephants," a dangerous and unprecedented stunt
teaming two powerful natural enemies. Years later, he pushed that idea a step
further when he trained one of his elephants, Congo, to carry a tiger named Prince
on its back. "My special trick" is what Gebel-Williams calls that one.

"Two years I practice with the tiger and the elephant," he says, his German   8
accent still thick after twenty-one years in the United States.

"This act will never happen again. No one else takes the time. Young trainers **9** now are too rushed. They think, 'You practice every day, you see nothing happen, you give up.' But you want to do it right, then you do it a little every day, and then do it a little more after that. Nothing happens fast with animals. This I know from experience, and experience comes only with age. I am a better animal trainer now than when I was young because, I think, you get better when you're older."

Gebel-Williams's skill with animals—he is the first man to win the prize for the **10** best circus act—was what caught the attention of Irvin Feld, the president and producer of Ringling Bros. and Barnum and Bailey. Gebel-Williams agreed to work for Feld, but only on the condition that Feld also buy Circus Williams and its thirty-member staff, to whom he felt a deep sense of loyalty.

Some of the Circus Williams crew is still with Gebel-Williams, along with newer **11** animal handlers who speak to the elephants with the same mixture of German and Hindi commands that the Circus Williams handlers use.

"I call it speaking Gebel to them," said animal handler Jeff Steele, who **12** reveres Gebel-Williams and his son, Mark Oliver Gebel.

"Gunther is the best boss I've ever had. He's tough, yeah, and tolerant. The **13** guy is incredible, he really is. He'll tell you that any problems are always the people's fault, never the animal's."

"That's right," says Gebel-Williams, whose muscular arms are a road map of **14** more than four hundred scars, all "from my own mistakes and being stupid." He has scars from being too close to tigers during a stunt, from the time a sick tiger lashed at him when it was startled by a doctor's injection, and from countless "stupid mistakes" during practice sessions.

Several years ago in Cincinnati, as Congo and Prince were making their **15** entrance, the curtain was hanging too low and grazed the tiger's head. Prince leaped from the elephant's back, ran behind a bench where a clown's mother and father were sitting, and put one massive paw on the woman's back, catching its claws—a tiger's claws don't retract—in her sweater. Gebel-Williams told her to stay calm, and she froze, as he unhooked the paw and coaxed Prince out from the bench.

Gebel-Williams's success with his animals depends on mutual trust; the **16** relationship is more mental than physical. "The most important thing is the respect I have for the animals and the respect they have for me," Gebel-Williams says.

When Gebel-Williams retires next year, the tigers will go with him. Gebel- **17** Williams has taught no one to handle them. His son, Mark Oliver Gebel, will take over the elephant act, but he will do it his father's way. That includes working alongside the animals for up to fifteen hours a day. Why will Gebel-Williams's son follow in his father's footsteps? "He will do it my way. When you have earned respect from an animal, and the animal knows to do things in a certain way, then you have to do things that way. These elephants have been with me twenty years or more. They must have respect."

(Adapted from the *Denver Post,* October 1, 1989.)

QUESTIONS

Now write your answers to the questions from the beginning of the reading.

1. Why is this an important time for Gunther Gebel-Williams?

_____

2. Why is Gebel-Williams important to the circus?

_____

3. What was Gebel-Williams's special trick with animals? Which animals?

_____

_____

4. Will someone continue Gebel-Williams's work after he stops working for the circus?

_____

5. What does Gebel-Williams think is most important in training animals?

_____

_____

COMPARISON

Compare the circus you described with the circus Gebel-Williams works in. The article does not include much specific information about the Ringling Bros. and Barnum and Bailey Circus, so you may not know exactly how it compares with the circus you saw. First, list three or four differences that you know about:

The circus you saw: The Ringling Bros. Circus:

_____   _____

_____   _____

_____   _____

_____   _____

Now list three or four differences that you think might exist:

The circus you saw: The Ringling Bros. Circus:

_____   _____

_____   _____

_____   _____

_____   _____

SUMMARIZING

Write a short sentence that summarizes each paragraph in the reading.

Example:
Paragraph 1   *Gunther Gebel-Williams jumped out of his trailer.*

Paragraph 2 _____

Paragraph 3 _____

Paragraph 4 _____

Paragraph 5 _____

Paragraph 6 _____

Paragraph 7 _____

Paragraph 8 _____

Paragraph 9 _____

Paragraph 10 _____

Paragraph 11 _____

Paragraph 12 _____

Paragraph 13 _____

Paragraph 14 _____

Paragraph 15 _____

Paragraph 16 _____

Paragraph 17 _____

VOCABULARY EXERCISE

1. In paragraph 1 there is a word that means "jumping." Write that word here:

_____

2. In paragraph 2 there is a word that means "takes hold with the hand." Write that word here: _____

3. In paragraph 2 there is a word that means "throws." Write that word here:

_____

4. In paragraph 4 there is a word that means "newspapers, radio, television, etc." Write that word here: _____

5. In paragraph 4 there is a word that means "stopping work." Write that word here: _____

6. In paragraph 6 there is a word that means "made someone else's child one's own child." Write that word here: _____

7. In paragraph 7 there is a word that means "better or best." Write that word here: _____

8. In paragraph 7 there is a word that means "never done before." Write that word here: _____

9. In paragraph 10 there is a phrase that means "made someone notice." Write that phrase here: _____

_____

(Continued at top of next page)

10. In paragraph 10 there is a word that means "staying with and supporting someone." Write that word here: _____

11. In paragraph 13 there is a word that means "hard to believe." Write that word here: _____

12. In paragraph 14 there is a word that means "surprised." Write that word here:

_____

L O N G   R E A D I N G   3

ANIMAL RIGHTS, HUMAN WRONGS?

Answer the following questions:

Is it acceptable to hurt a cat or monkey until it goes insane or dies?

Yes _____   No _____

Is it acceptable to put chemicals in the eyes of rabbits until they go blind?

Yes _____   No _____

Is it acceptable to turn animals into drug addicts?

Yes _____   No _____

Is it acceptable to make chimpanzees sit alone in cages for months while they are being used for scientific research?

Yes _____   No _____

Should there be any limits on how people use animals?

Yes _____   No _____

These are questions that are being asked more and more frequently. A growing number of people all over the world believe that animals have rights and that there should be limits on what humans can do to animals. Some feel that we can continue to use animals for scientific research and for food and clothing, but that we should not cause more pain to animals than we need to. Others have stronger beliefs and feel that humans have no right to do anything to an animal that they would not do to another human.

All of these people are part of what is referred to as the animals rights movement. The movement has objected to the use of animals in scientific research, especially when that research causes pain and death to the animals, and to the use of animals as "unnecessary" beauty and decoration aids, such as in fur coats. Many members of the movement believe that humans have no greater right to life and comfort than a dog, rabbit, monkey, or rat has.

Opposed to the animal rights movement are a large number of scientists and researchers who use animals in their research, many ordinary people who believe that such research is necessary and beneficial, and individuals who simply like to wear fur coats and ivory jewelry. Many of these people believe that animals were put on the earth for use by humans and that we would be foolish not to use animals to increase our scientific knowledge and for food and clothing.

The focus of the debate is the use of animals in scientific research. Animals, especially rats and mice, dogs, cats, and various kinds of monkeys or primates such as chimpanzees and rhesus monkeys, are used to help scientists understand diseases and to develop drugs and treatments to cure diseases. Over 15 million animals are used for research in the United States every year. Smallpox and polio have been essentially wiped out using vaccines developed through animal research.

But animal rights activists argue that animals are not just being used, they are being abused. The activists describe how laboratory animals are often kept alone and frightened in dirty cages, how animals are given painful electrical shocks in learning experiments, how rabbits are tied down and harsh cosmetics inserted into their eyes, and how primates are drugged or injured and then killed to see the effects of the drugs or injury. Many animal rights activists believe that research can continue but with greater care for the animals' welfare. Others would like to see a complete ban on the use of animals in research.

The following articles were written by two people on opposite sides of this question, one who believes that research using animals is beneficial and should continue and another who believes that the use of animals in research should be restricted.

> **Note:** The following articles are taken directly from *Newsweek* magazine. They may be difficult, but you should be able to understand the main ideas.

PREREADING ACTIVITY

Read the article on page 174 slowly and carefully (taking about twenty minutes) to find the answers to these questions:

1. Who is the writer, and why is she interested in the use of animals in research?
2. What is the writer's opinion about the use of animals?
3. What reasons does she give for her belief?
4. Do you think the writer wants any limit on the use of animals in research?

Is a Lab Rat's Fate More Important than a Child's?

by Jane McCabe

1   I see the debate about using animals in medical research in stark terms. If you had to choose between saving a very cute dog or my equally cute, blond, brown-eyed daughter, whose life would you choose? It's not a difficult choice, is it? My daughter has cystic fibrosis. Her only hope for a normal life is that researchers, some of them using animals, will find a cure. Don't misunderstand. It's not that I don't love animals, it's just that I love Claire more.

2   Nine years ago I had no idea that I would be joining the fraternity of those who have a vital interest in seeing that medical research continues. I was a very pregnant woman in labor; with my husband beside me I gave birth to a 7-pound 1-ounce daughter. It all seemed so easy. But for the next four months she could not gain weight. She was a textbook case of failure to thrive. Finally a hospital test of the salt content in her sweat led to the diagnosis of cystic fibrosis.

3   The doctor gave us a little reason for hope. "Your daughter will not have a long life, but for most of the time, it will be a good life. Her life expectancy is about 13 years, though it could be longer or shorter. As research continues, we're keeping them alive longer."

4   "As research continues." It's not a lot to rely on but what's our alternative? We haven't waited passively. We learned how to take care of our little girl; her medical problems affect her digestion and lungs. We protected her from colds, learned about supplemental vitamins and antibiotics. We moved to California where the winters aren't so harsh and the cold and flu season isn't so severe. Our new doctor told us that the children at his center were surviving, on the average, to age 21. So far, our daughter is doing well. She is a fast runner and plays a mean first base. She loves her friends and is, in general, a happy little girl. All things considered, I feel very lucky.

5   How has research using animals helped those with CF? Three times a day my daughter uses enzymes from the pancreas of pigs to digest her food. She takes antibiotics tested on rats before they are tried on humans. As an adult, she will probably develop diabetes and need insulin—a drug developed by research on dogs and rabbits. If she ever needs a heart-lung transplant, one might be possible because of the cows that surgeons practiced on. There is no animal model to help CF research, but once the CF gene is located, new gene-splicing techniques may create a family of mice afflicted with the disease. Researchers would first learn to cure the mice with drugs, then cautiously try with humans.

6   There are only about 10,000 people with CF in the United States. But the number of people dependent on research is much larger. Walk with me through Children's Hospital at Stanford University: here are the youngsters fighting cancer, rare genetic illnesses, immunological diseases. Amid their laughter and desperate attempts to retain a semblance of childhood, there is suffering.

7   **Human suffering:** I think the motivation of animal-rights activists is to cut down on the suffering in this world, but I have yet to hear them acknowledge that people—young and old—suffer, too. Why is a laboratory rat's fate more poignant than that of an incurably ill child?

8   There are advocates for animals who only seek to cut down on "unnecessary research." They don't specify how to decide what is unnecessary, but they do create an atmosphere in which doing medical research is seen as distasteful work. I think that's wrong. Researchers should be thanked, not hassled.

9   Every time I see a bumper sticker that says "Lab animals never have a nice day," a fantasy plays in my brain. I get out of my car, tap on the driver's window and ask to talk. In my fantasy, the other driver gets out, we find a coffee shop and I show her photos of my kids. I ask her if she has ever visited Children's Hospital. I am so eloquent that her eyes fill with tears and she promises to think of the children who are wasting away as she considers the whole complicated issue of suffering.

10   I have other fantasies, too, that a cure is found for what ails my daughter, that she marries and gives us some grandchildren, and does great work in her chosen profession, which at this moment appears to be cartooning or computer programming. We can still hope—as long as the research continues.

Jane McCabe lives with her husband and children in northern California.

Now write your answers to the questions from the beginning of the article.

1. Who is the writer, and why is she interested in the use of animals in research?

_____

2. What is the writer's opinion about the use of animals?

_____

3. What reasons does she give for her belief?

_____

4. Do you think the writer wants any limit on the use of animals in research?

_____

Based on what you have read so far, would you change any of your answers to the questions at the beginning of this section?

Is it acceptable to hurt a cat or monkey until it goes insane or dies?

Yes _____   No _____

Is it acceptable to put chemicals in the eyes of rabbits until they go blind?

Yes _____   No _____

Is it acceptable to turn animals into drug addicts?   Yes _____   No _____

Is it acceptable to make chimpanzees sit alone in cages for months while they are being used for scientific research?

Yes _____   No _____

Should there be any limits on how people use animals?   Yes _____   No _____

Now read the article on page 176 slowly and carefully (again taking about twenty minutes) to find the answers to these questions:

1. What is the writer's position about the use of animals?
2. Does he believe that using animals has any benefits at all?
3. What problem does the writer think results from poor treatment of laboratory animals?
4. What is the writer's attitude toward the argument about the use of animals in medical research? What does he hope will be the end of the argument?

We Must Find Alternatives to Animals in Research   by Roger Caras

1   I believe that animals have rights which, although different from our own, are just as inalienable. I believe animals have the right not to have pain, fear or physical deprivation inflicted upon them by us. Even if they are on the way to the slaughterhouse, animals have the right to food and water and shelter if it is needed. They have the right not to be brutalized in any way as food resources, for entertainment or any other purpose.

2   Since animals must be classified as property if we are to have the power of life and death over them (and we must, even over our pets), there is a vast philosophical/legal rift to be negotiated. No other property has rights, yet animals must. It is going to take some fine legal minds to work out the details so that we can get across that gulch.

3   One of the most difficult problems is our unrelenting use of animals in biomedical research. Until recently the arguments between biomedical researchers and the humane movement centered on the conditions under which laboratory animals are maintained. Lately, in keeping with our "age of activism," it has become a raging name-calling contest over whether one species, ours, has the right to use other species to solve our own health problems. If tens of millions of people elect to smoke and expose themselves to the risk of cancer and heart disease, do we have the right to subject animals that would never smoke to those same cancers and heart diseases?

4   A great many researchers I have met would love to have alternatives. They are against vivisection in spirit but believe that today's research protocols require—and grant money goes to—research involving animals. Often they are right. What's more, the use of animals in research is not limited to the good of humans. Vaccines used on animals were developed using animals. Animal-rights advocates who decry using animals for research on human diseases have not made it clear what models should have been used for canine distemper, parvovirus or feline leukemia.

5   Animal-rights activists say that far too little effort has gone into seeking substitute methods such as cell culture and computer modeling. They are right. Finding a substitute for animals in research has only recently become an imperative in the scientific commu-

nity. And that change has coincided with a change in the techniques employed by the militant animal-rights movement. When leaflets and picket signs were replaced by night raiders and bombers, science sat up and paid attention. Personally, I decry terrorism as the solution to any problem.

6   **Cruel boredom:** Many laboratories provide too little in the way of creature comforts (no pun intended) for laboratory animals. That has to change and in many places it is. Jane Goodall has fought to upgrade the psychological environment provided for chimpanzees. For an animal as bright as a chimp (its genetic package varies from our own by no more than 1 percent, most researchers agree), boredom and lack of social interaction is nothing less than cruelty, according to Goodall.

7   Much of the research done on chimps involves their immune systems, current work on AIDS being an obvious example. Since scientists know that stress alters any animal's power to respond to invading organisms, why do they stress chimps by confining them in isolation when the research protocol doesn't demand it?

8   What has happened is analogous to current geopolitical problems. Everybody is so angry at everybody else nobody is really listening. The animal-rights groups are at odds with each other. That could be because they are all looking for the same membership dollars, the same bequests. Then, of course, there are the antivivisectionists vs. the provivisectionists. They are so busy shrieking at each other no one can be heard.

9   One day animals will not be used in the laboratory. How soon that day comes depends on how soon people stop screaming and make the search for alternatives a major research imperative. As long as conferences on the subject sound like feeding time in the monkey house, monkeys along with millions of other animals are going to stay right where they are now—in the laboratory.

Roger Caras reports on animals and the environment for ABC-TV News.

Now write your answers to the questions from the beginning of the reading.

1. What is the writer's position about the use of animals?

_____

2. Does he believe that using animals has any benefits at all?

_____

3. What problem does the writer think results from poor treatment of laboratory animals?

_____

_____

4. What is the writer's attitude toward the argument about the use of animals in medical research? What does he hope will be the end of the argument?

_____

_____

_____

_____

Now would you change any of your answers to the questions at the beginning of this section?

Is it acceptable to hurt a cat or monkey until it goes insane or dies?

Yes _____   No _____

Is it acceptable to put chemicals in the eyes of rabbits until they go blind?

Yes _____   No _____

Is it acceptable to turn animals into drug addicts?

Yes _____   No _____

Is it acceptable to make chimpanzees sit alone in cages for months while they are being used for scientific research?

Yes _____   No _____

Should there be any limits on how people use animals?

Yes _____   No _____

COMPARISON

Working in pairs or in groups, compare the two articles by answering the following questions.

1. What facts are found in both articles?

_____

_____

_____

2. What facts are found only in the first article?

_____

_____

_____

3. What facts are found only in the second article?

_____

_____

_____

REASONS AND OPINIONS

Work in groups of three or four, and list five reasons why we should use animals for research. Then list five reasons why we should not use animals for research. Write the reasons even if you do not agree with them. When all the groups are finished, compare your lists. Add to your lists any reasons you hear that you did not think of. After you have considered all the reasons, decide what your opinion on the subject is and write it in the space provided on page 180.

Five reasons for using animals:

    1. _____

    2. _____

    3. _____

    4. _____

    5. _____

Other reasons for using animals:

    6. _____

    7. _____

    8. _____

    9. _____

    10. _____

Five reasons against using animals:

    1. _____

    2. _____

    3. _____

    4. _____

    5. _____

Other reasons against using animals:

    6. _____

    7. _____

    8. _____

    9. _____

    10. _____

Your opinion about using animals for scientific research:

_____

_____

_____

_____

CHAPTER REVIEW

In this chapter you have read about exotic animals, sharks, a circus animal trainer, and animal rights. Answer the following questions about the readings. Work alone and answer for yourself. Most of the questions do not have one correct answer; the answers are your opinion or are true for you. When you are finished, discuss your answers with your instructor and the rest of the class.

1. Which reading did you learn the most from? Why?

_____

_____

2. Write five pieces of information that you learned from reading this chapter:

a. _____

_____

b. _____

_____

c. _____

_____

d. _____

_____

e. _____

_____

3. Which reading was the most interesting? Why?

_____

_____

4. Which reading was the easiest to read? Why?

_____

_____

5. Which reading was the most difficult to read? Why?

_____

_____

6. Which reading had the most personal experience or opinion in it?

_____

7. Which reading had the most research in it?

_____

Now that you have read and thought about animals, write three questions that you still have about animals.

Example:
**Where can wolves be found in North America?** _____

1. _____

2. _____

3. _____

Working in groups or as a class, agree on three questions that you think are the most interesting. Then, as a group, try to decide where you might find the answers to these questions. You might need to look in a particular book or encyclopedia, or interview a particular person. If there is time, go as a group and find the answers to the questions.

WRITING OR SPEAKING SUMMARY

Choose one of the following topics. Then write at least a page on that topic or prepare to talk to the rest of the class about it. Use the information and language you have learned in this chapter, and your own ideas and information you collect from elsewhere.

1. What benefits are there to keeping animals as pets? What is wrong with keeping animals as pets?

2. Compare two animals as pets. For example, which make better pets—dogs or cats? Why?

3. Do you believe that animals can think? Give reasons for your opinion.

4. Animals and people are working together in new and interesting ways. Dogs can be taught to help deaf people as well as blind people, and dolphins (marine

mammals) are helping in underwater research. Describe a way in which animals and people can work together that was not mentioned in this chapter. It may be a way that already exists or some way that you would like to suggest. Include information about the animal, the kind of work it would do, and the kind of training it would need.

READING JOURNAL

List the outside reading you did while studying this chapter. (Include the title or type of material, length, topic or subject, and where you found the material.)

_____

_____

_____

Write a journal entry for this outside reading. Your instructor will want to look at your journal and may ask you to tell the rest of the class about something you read. In your journal you might answer the following questions. Or you can write about anything else you felt or learned as you were reading.

What was the most interesting thing you read? Why was it interesting?

What was the least interesting thing you read? Why was it not interesting?

What is one piece of information you learned about animals from your outside reading?

Was the reading you did difficult or easy? Why do you think it was difficult or easy?

Do you have questions about animals that you can find the answers to by reading? What are they? What can you read to find the answers?

Did you enjoy the outside reading you did while you studied this chapter? Why or why not?

Chapter
7

WATER AND US

Water, water everywhere and not a drop to drink.
—Adapted from "The Ancient Mariner"
by Samuel Taylor Coleridge

INTRODUCTION

This chapter will be a little different from the other chapters in the book. One new feature is that all of the long readings are taken from other publications. Also, some of the activities you will be doing are unlike the activities in previous chapters. Because the readings are longer and a little more difficult, there will be fewer activities. At the end of the chapter you will do a short research project about water using your reading and writing abilities and some outside information sources.

Let's begin, however, by looking at the expression at the top of this page. This expression is from a famous poem written in English. Working with a partner or in groups, decide what the sentence means, who might have said it, and where and when. Write your guess here:

_____

_____

_____

_____

_____

_____

Now compare your guess with the guesses of the other groups in the class. As a class, decide which is the best. You might want to find the line in the original poem to see what Coleridge meant when he wrote the line.

OUTSIDE READING

Doing outside reading about water will help you to understand this chapter better. Science magazines and textbooks are good sources of basic information about water. However, like water itself, information about water can appear almost anywhere.

Take a few minutes in class and suggest outside readings about water and where to find them. Write on the lines below some good suggestions that you hear.

_____

_____

_____

_____

_____

Be sure to write about your outside reading in your Reading Journal.

INFORMATION GATHERING

On the lines below, list as many ways as you can think of that you use water during a usual day. You might think of ways that you yourself use water, or ways that someone else uses water to help you do something. Work alone and write for five minutes. When you are finished, your instructor will ask the students with the longest lists to read them aloud. If you hear uses that you did not think of, add them to your list.

_____

_____

_____

_____

_____

_____
_____
_____
_____
_____
_____
_____
_____

S H O R T   R E A D I N G

PREREADING ACTIVITY

The following reading contains some general information about water. First, look over the questions and see if you can answer any of them. Then read carefully and slowly to find the answers to all the questions.

1. What percentage of a human being is water?
2. What is one way that water is useful?
3. What is one way that water is dangerous?
4. What percentage of the people in less developed countries do not have enough clean water to drink?
5. What percentage of human illness is related to water?
6. How can water cause problems for agriculture?

Water

Water is the most common substance on earth. It is in the air that we breathe and in the ground that we walk on. It fills oceans, rivers, and lakes.   1

Every living thing consists mostly of water. A human being is about 65 percent water, an elephant about 70 percent, a potato about 80 percent, and a tomato an amazing 95 percent.   2

Water is both dangerous and useful. In rain and floods, water can damage our buildings and the land we live on and even kill. But we need to drink water. We   3 also use it in cooking and for bathing. Water carries away our waste products and irrigates our fields.

Although the supply of fresh water available in the world is constantly being **4** renewed, usable water is not evenly distributed. Over half of the people in less developed countries do not have clean water to drink, and three quarters have no sanitation. Yet more than 75 percent of all human illness is related to lack of clean water and sanitation.

Water is necessary for agriculture, yet when irrigation is not managed well it **5** can ruin the land it is supposed to improve by turning it into a salty desert. Water is required for factories and the production of electricity, but dangerous wastes from industry can turn rivers into sewers and rain into an acid shower that can kill a lake and destroy a forest.

There is as much water on earth today as there ever has been or ever will be. **6** But that water needs to be used carefully and well. If we understand where water comes from and how to use it safely and well, future supplies of water will be available for our children and for their children.

QUESTIONS

Now write your answers to the questions from the beginning of the reading.

1. What percentage of a human being is water?

_____

2. What is one way that water is useful?

_____

3. What is one way that water is dangerous?

_____

4. What percentage of the people in less developed countries do not have enough clean water to drink?

_____

5. What percentage of human illness is related to water?

_____

6. How can water cause problems for agriculture?

_____

Did you change any of your answers after reading the passage? Compare your answers with the answers other students in the class gave. Did you all agree on the answers? If not, why not?

L O N G   R E A D I N G   1

PREREADING ACTIVITY

The following reading is taken from a science textbook. It is the beginning of a chapter on fresh water. Scan the reading quickly (in about ten minutes) to find answers to the following questions:

1. How many parts are there in the reading?
2. What is the subject of each part?
3. What is the water cycle?
4. What is running water? What are some examples of running water?
5. What is standing water? What are some examples of standing water?

FRESH WATER ON THE EARTH'S SURFACE

Water is one of the most abundant substances on the earth's surface. A casual glance at a world map might make you think that the earth has enough water to meet the needs of living things forever. After all, oceans cover more than 70 percent of the earth's surface. In fact, about 90 percent of the earth's water is found in the oceans. But most of the ocean water cannot be used by living things because it contains salt. The salt would have to be removed before the water could be used. **1**

Fresh water makes up about 3 percent of the earth's water. But most of this fresh water cannot be used because it is locked up in ice, mainly in icecaps near the North and South Poles and in glaciers. In fact, only 15 percent of the earth's fresh water is available for use by living things. This very small percent represents the earth's total available supply of fresh water. With such a limited supply, you might wonder why the earth does not run out of fresh water. It does not because the supply of fresh water is continuously being renewed. **2**

THE WATER CYCLE

Most of the fresh water on the earth's surface is found in moving water and in standing water. Rivers, streams, and springs are moving water. Ponds, lakes, and swampy wetlands are standing water. **3**

Water moves among these sources of fresh water, the salty oceans, the air, and the land in an endless cycle. A cycle is a continuous chain of events. The *water cycle* is the continuous movement of water from the oceans and freshwater sources to the air and land and then back to the oceans. The water cycle, also called the hydrologic cycle, constantly renews the earth's supply of fresh water. Three main steps make up the water cycle. **4**

The first step of the water cycle involves the heat energy of the sun. This energy causes the water on the surface of the earth to change to a vapor, or gas. This process is called *evaporation*. Enormous amounts of water evaporate from the oceans. Water also evaporates from freshwater sources, as well as from the soil, animals, and plants. The water vapor is then carried by winds over the land and oceans. **5**

The second step of the water cycle involves a process called *condensation*. Condensation is the process by which vapor changes back into a liquid. For condensation to occur, the air containing the water vapor must be cooled. And this is exactly what happens as the warm air close to the earth's surface rises. The warm air cools and can no longer hold as much water vapor. Most of the water vapor condenses into droplets of water that form clouds. But these clouds are not "salty" clouds. When the water evaporates from oceans, the salt is left behind. **6**

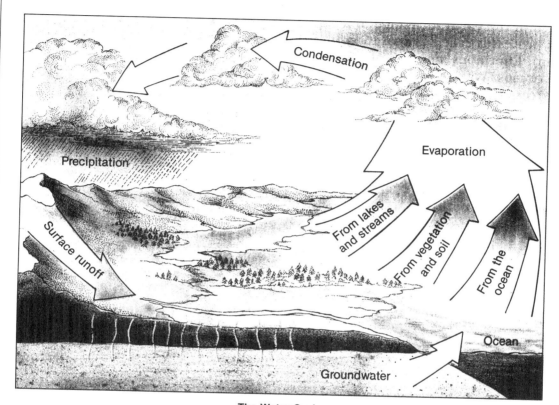

The Water Cycle

During the third step of the water cycle, the water returns to the earth in the form   7
of rain, snow, sleet, or hail. This process is called *precipitation*. Precipitation occurs
when the water droplets that form a cloud become too numerous and too heavy to
remain floating in the air. Water that falls to the earth as rain, snow, sleet, or hail is
fresh water.

After the water falls to the earth, some of the water returns to the atmosphere   8
through evaporation. Then the cycle begins again. As a result of the water cycle, the
earth's supply of fresh water is constantly renewed.

Some of the remaining water that is returned to the earth may run off into ponds,   9
lakes, streams, rivers, or oceans. Some may soak into the ground and become
groundwater. Groundwater is the water that remains in the ground. At some point, the

groundwater flows underground to the oceans. This water then reenters the water cycle.

RUNNING WATER

Rivers and streams are very important sources of fresh water. Many cities and towns were built near rivers and streams. The water was used for irrigating, generating electric power, and drinking. Industry and commerce depend on rivers for transporting supplies and equipment. Rivers and streams are also used for fishing, boating, and swimming. 10

Rain and melted snow that do not evaporate or soak into the soil flow into rivers and streams. The water entering a river or stream after a heavy rain or during a spring thaw of snow or ice is called *surface runoff*. 11

The amount of surface runoff is affected by several factors. One factor is the type of soil the rain or snow falls on. Some soils soak up more water than others. Such soils have more space between their particles. The space between particles of soil is called the *pore space*. The more pore space a soil has, the more water it will hold. The condition of the soil also affects the amount of runoff. If the soil is dry, it will soak up a great deal of water and thus reduce the surface runoff. 12

The number of plants growing in the soil also affects the amount of runoff. Plant roots absorb water from the soil. In areas where there are many plants, large amounts of water are absorbed. So the runoff there is less. The seasons are another factor in the amount of runoff. There will be more runoff in rainy seasons and in the spring, when large amounts of snow are melting. 13

A land area in which surface runoff drains into a river or system of rivers is called a *watershed*. Watersheds can be very small or very large. Some watersheds cover millions of acres and drain their water into the oceans. Watersheds prevent floods and water shortages by controlling the amount of water that feeds into streams and rivers. They also help to provide a steady flow of fresh water to the oceans. 14

Many rivers are sources of fresh water. The amount of water in a river and the speed at which the water flows affect the usefulness of a river as a source of fresh water. Rivers that move quickly carry a lot of water. But because the water is moving rapidly, they also carry a large amount of soil, pebbles, and other sediments. The water in these rivers often looks cloudy. Slow-moving rivers do not churn up as much sediment. Their water is clearer. These rivers are better sources of fresh water. 15

In recent years, pollution has had an effect on the usefulness of rivers as sources of fresh water. If a river has many factories along its banks that are discharging wastes into the river, the water will become polluted. The water must be cleaned before it can be used. Some rivers are so heavily polluted that they cannot be used as sources of fresh water. 16

STANDING WATER

Within a watershed, some of the surface runoff gets caught in low places. Standing bodies of fresh water are formed there. These standing bodies of water are called lakes and ponds, depending on their size. 17

Like streams and rivers, lakes and ponds continually receive runoff from the land. The runoff keeps them from drying up. These standing bodies of water are important sources of fresh water. Moosehead Lake, in Maine, is a natural source of fresh water. It is 56 kilometers long and 3 to 16 kilometers wide. The pine-forested shores of the lake can hold huge amounts of water from rains and melting snow. The water is released slowly to the lake, so flooding is not likely. During times of drought, the lake holds a huge supply of water in reserve. 18

LAKES AND PONDS

Lakes are usually deep depressions in the earth's crust that have filled with fresh water. Rain, melting snow, water from springs and rivers, and surface runoff fill these depressions. A lake is sometimes formed when there is a natural obstruction, or blocking, of a river or stream. Lakes can be found in many places on the earth. They are most frequently found at relatively high altitudes and in areas where glaciers were once present. 19

Ponds are shallow depressions in the earth's crust that have filled with fresh water. They are usually smaller and not as deep as lakes. Sunlight can penetrate to the bottom of a pond. Lakes, however, have some very deep areas that sunlight cannot reach. Ponds also have more plant growth than lakes. 20

RESERVOIRS

The most frequently used sources of fresh water are artificial lakes known as *reservoirs*. A reservoir is built by damming a stream or river in a low-lying area. When the stream or river is dammed, water backs up behind the dam. Reservoirs have been built near cities and towns and in mountainous regions throughout the country. 21

Reservoirs serve several purposes. They help control water flow during periods of heavy rain and runoff. This prevents flooding. During periods of little rain or runoff, reservoirs store water. They serve as sources of drinking water for nearby towns and cities and provide irrigation water for farms. Reservoirs can also be used in the generation of electrical power. The water stored behind the dams can be moved through hydroelectric plants. These plants convert the energy of the running water into electrical power. 22

A reservoir, however, cannot be used for all purposes at the same time. Why is this   23
so? Suppose a reservoir is being used to store water. To use it also in the generation
of electricity, the water would have to be drawn from the reservoir and moved through
the hydroelectric plant. The reservoir would no longer be storing water.

Section Review

1. What are the major sources of fresh water on the earth's surface?
2. What is the water cycle?
3. Why are watersheds important?
4. Explain why a reservoir cannot be used to control flooding and store water at the same time.

(From Coble, C., D. Rice, K. Walla, and E. Murray. 1988. *Earth Science*. Englewood Cliffs, N.J.: Prentice-Hall.)

QUESTIONS

Now write your answers to the questions from the beginning of the reading.

1. How many parts are there in the reading?

_____

2. What is the subject of each part?

_____

3. What is the water cycle?

_____

_____

4. What is running water? What are some examples of running water?

_____

_____

5. What is standing water? What are some examples of standing water?

_____

_____

Read the selection again carefully and slowly, taking about twenty minutes. Be able to identify the most important information in the reading.

FILL-IN-THE-BLANK

Fill in the blanks in the following passage with information from the reading.

Water is one of the most abundant substances on the earth's surface. Oceans cover

_____ of the earth's surface, and about _____ of the earth's
(1)   (2)

water is found in oceans. Fresh water makes up only about _____ of the
(3)

earth's water, but most of it cannot be used because it is _____.
(4)

_____ water and _____ water are the forms in which most fresh
(5)   (6)

water is found. Water moves among these sources of fresh water in a process called

the _____.
(7)

The first step of the water cycle is called _____ and occurs when heat
(8)

energy changes water to a _____. _____, the second step of the
(9)   (10)

cycle, is when water _____ to a liquid. Rain, snow, sleet, and hail are forms
(11)

of _____, the third step in the cycle.
(12)

Groundwater is water that soaks into the ground and _____ there.
(13)

Rivers and streams are the most important types of running water. They get most

of their water from _____. The _____ from which water runs
(14)   (15)

into rivers and streams is a watershed. Rivers often carry a lot of sediment in

the form of _____ and _____, and also pollution from
(16)   (17)

_____ and other wastes.
(18)

Lakes, ponds, and reservoirs are all forms of standing water. Lakes and ponds are

_____, and reservoirs are _____. Reservoirs are built for the
(19)   (20)

purposes of controlling _____, providing _____, and generating
(21)   (22)

_____.
(23)

APPLYING THE TEXT

I'm Thirsty

An average person needs about 25 liters of water a day to live. How much water

will each person need in a year? _____

How much water will your class need a day to live? _____

How much in a year? _____

Hydroelectric Power

The total potential hydroelectric power of the world is 2.25 billion kilowatts. But only 363 million kilowatts of this is being utilized. The United States uses one sixth of the world's electric power. Calculate the percentage of the world's potential hydroelectric power that is being used. Then calculate the percentage of the world's water power now used in the United States.

DEFINITIONS

The following exercise is taken from the same textbook as the readings. Based on what you have read, write definitions of the following words:

Fresh water:

_____

_____

Water cycle:

_____

_____

Evaporation:

_____

_____

Condensation:

_____

_____

Precipitation:

_____

_____

Groundwater:

_____

_____

Surface runoff:

_____

_____

Watershed:

_____

_____

Reservoir:

_____

_____

USING INFORMATION

Look again at the water uses you listed at the beginning of this chapter, and write *S* before each use that could have been done with salt water. When everyone has finished, each student should present his or her results to the class. Then make a combined list of possible uses for salt water in your area. How long is the list?

PREPARING A REPORT

Work in three groups. One group should try to identify the source or sources of fresh water in the area where you are studying. You might need to telephone the local water department to be sure of your information. If there is more than one source of water, rank the sources in order of the amount of water that comes from each source. Finally, if precipitation affects the availability of water in the area, try to determine what form of precipitation is most important.

The second group should identify the major uses of water in the community (for example, residential, industrial, hydroelectric, agriculture). Try to determine the order of importance of use. The group might need to consult outside sources of information such as the city or area government or water department.

The third group should determine what problems exist with water and water usage in the area. These may be availability, cleanliness, pollution, and cost. Again, try to rank the problems in order of importance. Outside information sources may be necessary.

Each group can write a summary of its results or report the results to the class orally. The written reports can be combined into a class report project.

L O N G   R E A D I N G   2

PREREADING ACTIVITY

The following reading is taken from the same science textbook as the reading on fresh water. This is from the chapter on salt water. Before you begin reading, the instructor will divide the class into groups. Each group should name as many countries as possible that border on the Pacific Ocean and the Atlantic Ocean. The time limit is ten minutes. When the time is finished, compare your lists. The group with the longest list of correct countries is the winner.

Now look over the reading quickly (in about ten minutes) to find the following information:

1. How many parts are there in the reading?
2. What is the subject of each part?
3. According to the reading, how many major oceans are there?
4. What is the most important salt in ocean water?
5. Where do ocean salts come from?
6. How many gases are commonly found in ocean water?
7. How many temperature zones are usually found in the ocean?

OCEANS OF THE WORLD

If you were to rename the earth, what would you call it? If you looked at its surface   1
features, you might call it Oceanus. About 71 percent of the earth's surface is covered
by ocean water. In fact, the ocean contains most of the earth's water—about 97
percent. Although people refer to separate oceans and seas, all of the oceans and seas
are part of one continuous body of water.

The Atlantic, Indian, and Pacific Oceans are the three major oceans. Smaller bodies   2
of ocean water, such as the Mediterranean Sea, the Black Sea, and the Arctic Ocean,
are considered part of the Atlantic Ocean. A sea is a part of an ocean that is nearly
surrounded by land.

The Pacific Ocean is the largest ocean. Its area and volume are greater than those   3
of the Atlantic and Indian Oceans combined. The Pacific Ocean is also the deepest
ocean. Its average depth is 3940 meters. The Atlantic Ocean is the second largest
ocean. It has an average depth of 3350 meters. The Indian Ocean is much smaller than
the Atlantic Ocean, but its average depth is greater.

The ocean, which is made of salt water, plays an important role in the water cycle.   4
During this cycle, the sun's rays heat the surface of the ocean. The heat causes the
water to evaporate. When the water evaporates, it enters the atmosphere as water
vapor. The salts the water contained remain in the ocean.

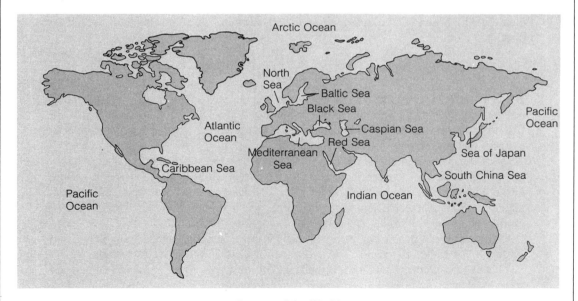

Oceans of the World

Winds carry much of the water vapor over land areas. Some of the water vapor in   5
the atmosphere condenses to form clouds. Under the right conditions, the water in
clouds falls as precipitation. This water is fresh water. Some of it runs into streams and
rivers that flow directly back to the ocean. Some of it seeps deep into the soil and rocks
to become part of the groundwater beneath the earth's surface. So indirectly, the ocean
is a source of fresh water for all living things.

Section Review

1. Name the three major oceans of the world.
2. What is the difference between an ocean and a sea?
3. Why is the ocean an indirect source of fresh water?

PROPERTIES OF OCEAN WATER

Ocean water is a mixture of gases and solids dissolved in pure water. Scientists who   6
study the ocean, or *oceanographers,* believe that ocean water contains all of the natural
elements on the earth. There are 90 elements known to exist in nature. About 85 of
these elements have already been found in ocean water. With advances in technology,
oceanographers hope to find the remaining elements.

Ocean water is about 96 percent pure water, or H_2O. So the most abundant   7
elements in ocean water are hydrogen and oxygen. The remaining 4 percent is
dissolved elements.

SALTS IN OCEAN WATER

Sodium chloride is the most abundant salt in ocean water. If you have ever   8
accidentally swallowed a mouthful of ocean water, you have probably recognized the
taste of sodium chloride. Sodium chloride is, in fact, common table salt. Sodium chloride
is made of the elements sodium and chloride.

Sodium chloride is one of the many salts dissolved in ocean water. Oceanographers   9
use the term *salinity* to describe the amount of dissolved salts in ocean water. Salinity
is the number of grams of dissolved salts in one kilogram of ocean water. When one
kilogram of ocean water evaporates, 35 grams of salts are left. Of these 35 grams, 27.2
grams are sodium chloride.

The salinity of ocean water is expressed in parts per thousand. It ranges between   10
33 and 37 parts per thousand. The average salinity is 35 parts per thousand.

The salts and other materials dissolved in ocean water come from several different   11
sources. One source is volcanic activity in the ocean. When volcanoes erupt, rock
material and gases spew forth. These substances are dissolved in ocean water. Chlorine
gas is one substance that is added to ocean water by volcanic action.

Another source is erosion of land areas by rivers and glaciers. As rivers and glaciers 12 pass over rocks and soil, they dissolve the salts in them. Sodium, magnesium, and potassium are probably carried to the ocean this way.

Wave action along shorelines is also a source of salts and other materials. As waves 13 pound the shorelines, they dissolve the salts contained in rocks along the coasts.

In many areas of the ocean, the salinity is about the same. But in other areas, 14 greater or lesser amounts of dissolved salts cause differences in salinity. There are several reasons for these differences. The salinity is much lower in areas where freshwater rivers flow into the ocean. This is especially true where major rivers such as the Mississippi, Amazon, and Congo flow into the ocean.

In warm ocean areas where there is little or no rainfall and much evaporation, the 15 amount of dissolved salts in the ocean water is greater than the average. The salinity is higher. The salinity is also higher in the polar regions. Here ocean water freezes, removing pure water and leaving the salts behind.

Scientists believe that the salinity of ocean water is also affected by animal life. 16 Animals such as clams and oysters use calcium salts to build their shells.

GASES IN OCEAN WATER

The most abundant gases dissolved in ocean water are nitrogen, carbon dioxide, 17 and oxygen. Two of these gases, carbon dioxide and oxygen, are vital to ocean life. Plants use carbon dioxide to make food. In the presence of sunlight, plants combine carbon dioxide with water to make simple sugars. During this process, oxygen is released into the water. Plants and animals use oxygen to break down food and provide energy for all life functions.

The amount of nitrogen, carbon dioxide, oxygen, and other gases in ocean water 18 varies with depth. Nitrogen, carbon dioxide, and oxygen are more abundant at the surface of ocean water. At the surface, sunlight easily penetrates and plant growth abounds. So there is a large amount of oxygen here.

The amount of dissolved gases is also affected by the temperature of the ocean 19 water. Warm water holds less dissolved gas than cold water. When ocean water cools, as in the polar regions, it sinks. It carries oxygen-rich water to the ocean depths. As a result, fish and other animals can live in the deepest parts of the ocean.

TEMPERATURE OF OCEAN WATER

The sun is the major source of heat for the ocean. Since solar energy is received 20 at the surface of ocean water, water temperatures are highest there. Motions of the ocean, such as waves and currents, mix the surface water and transfer the heat downward. The zone where the water is mixed by waves and currents is called the

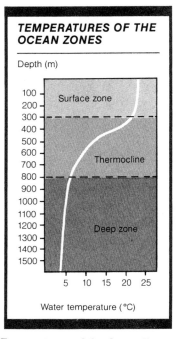

Temperatures of the Ocean Zones

surface zone. The surface zone extends to a depth of at least 100 meters. Sometimes it extends as deep as 400 meters.

Within a surface zone, the temperature remains fairly constant. It does not change 21 with depth. But the temperature of a surface zone does change with location and with season. Water near the equator is warmer than water in regions further north and south. And summer water temperatures are warmer than winter temperatures. For example, the summer water temperature near the surface of the Caribbean Sea may be 26°. Off the coast of England, it may be 15°.

Below the surface zone, the temperature of the water falls very rapidly. This zone 22 of rapid temperature change is called the *thermocline.* The thermocline does not have a specific depth. The season of the year and the flow of ocean currents affect its depth.

The thermocline exists because warm surface water does not mix easily with cold 23 deep water. The differences in the densities of the warm water and the cold water keep them from mixing. The less dense warm water floats on the denser cold water.

The thermocline is the transition zone between the surface zone and the *deep zone.* 24 The deep zone is an area of very cold water that extends from the bottom of the thermocline to depths of 400 meters or more. Within the deep zone, the temperature decreases slightly. At depths of more than 1500 meters, the temperature is about 4°C. So the temperature of most ocean water is just above freezing.

The three ocean zones are not found in the polar regions. In the Arctic and Antarctic Oceans, the surface waters are very cold. The temperature changes only slightly as the depth increases.   25

Section Review

1. What is the most abundant salt in ocean water?
2. What is salinity?
3. What are the most abundant gases in ocean water?
4. What are the three zones of the ocean? On what property of ocean water are these zones based?

(From Coble, C., D. Rice, K. Walla, and E. Murray. 1988. *Earth Science.* Englewood Cliffs, N.J.: Prentice-Hall.)

QUESTIONS

Now write your answers to the questions from the beginning of the reading.

1. How many parts are there in the reading?

_____

2. What is the subject of each part?

_____

3. According to the reading, how many major oceans are there?

_____

4. What is the most important salt in ocean water?

_____

5. Where do ocean salts come from?

_____

(Continued at top of next page)

6. How many gases are commonly found in ocean water?

_____

7. How many temperature zones are usually found in the ocean?

_____

Now read the selection more slowly and carefully, taking about twenty minutes.

SUMMARY WRITING

Write a short summary of the reading on salt water. When you are finished, work with two other students and compare your summaries. Did you all include the same information? Decide if any of your summaries leave out important information or include information that is not important.

COMPREHENSION QUESTIONS

Answer the following questions about the reading:

1. Name five seas of the world.

_____

_____

2. What role does the ocean play in the water cycle that you read about in the previous reading?

_____

_____

3. What are the two most abundant elements in sea water?

_____

4. What are the third and fourth most abundant elements in sea water?

_____

5. How many grams of table salt and fresh water are needed to make a solution with the same salinity as ocean water?

_____

6. Where do most of the sodium, magnesium, and potassium in the ocean come from?

_____

7. Why do ocean areas near major rivers have lower salinity than areas farther away from rivers?

_____

8. Why is there more oxygen at the surface of ocean water than in the ocean depths?

_____

9. In which depth or temperature zone of the ocean is there a rapid temperature change?

_____

10. Why is there no thermocline zone in the Arctic and Antarctic?

_____

APPLYING THE TEXT

The following two experiments are taken from the same textbook as the readings. If possible, you and a partner should do the experiments and then write a short description of what you did and what happened.

Experiment I: Relating Temperature and Salinity

1. Pour 100ml of hot tap water into a glass.
2. Add salt, one teaspoonful at a time, to the water. Stir the water after each addition. Stop adding salt when no more can be dissolved. Record the number of teaspoons of salt added.
3. Using 100ml of cold tap water, repeat steps 1 and 2. In which glass did more salt dissolve? What is the relationship between temperature and salinity?

Experiment II: Fresh Water from the Ocean

1. Using your knowledge of the properties of ocean water, including density, devise a procedure for obtaining fresh water from ocean water by freezing. Describe the steps.
2. Try out the procedure using a solution of 100ml of tap water and 3g of salt. Report your results.

EXTENDING THE TEXT

Using the information you have read about oceans, write a description of what the ocean would be like at a depth of 3000 meters.

Compare descriptions and see if yours has all the necessary information. Did you or anyone else use information that was not included in the reading? Where did that information come from? How can you be sure it is correct?

DEFINITIONS

Fill in each blank with the word that is defined in the sentence.

1. A part of an ocean that is nearly surrounded by land is a

_____.

2. A scientist who studies the ocean is called an _____.

3. The amount of salt in water is the water's _____.

4. _____ is the word we use to describe what happens when a solid becomes part of a liquid.

5. A zone of rapid temperature change is a _____.

L O N G   R E A D I N G   3

PREREADING ACTIVITY

Scan the following reading quickly (in about five minutes) to find answers to the following questions:

1. What problem does the article describe?
2. How many stages in the growth of cities are identified?

Cities Athirst

1   Today's giant cities sprawl across wide areas and have an impact on the environment far from their city centers. London, Paris, Mexico City, Amsterdam, Los Angeles, and many others have pushed out into fertile farmland and, in so doing, have transformed it into endless blocks of buildings. They have stretched their fingers of iron and concrete pipe many kilometers out into the countryside to capture the contents of distant streams and lakes. They have removed much of the vegetation within their own city boundaries, replacing the green of grass, shrubs, and trees with asphalt, concrete, and impervious rooftops.

2   All these actions have affected the urban environment and the water supplies upon which the city-dwellers depend.

3   Numerous events take place during the change of an uninhabited piece of ground into a city complete with streets, squares, subway tunnels, and statues. Three stages in a city's growth have an impact on the water supply of the growing city.

4   The first stage involves the removal of trees and other vegetation to make room for the initial homes, stores, and streets. This removal improves the local area's water supply slightly by reducing the amount of water once "lost" from the vegetation. The digging of wells to supply the city-dwellers also usually takes place during the first stage. This also affects the local water supply as the wells will usually lower the water table.

5   Streams in the new city will also be affected by sedimentation, or the filling of streams with soil. The construction of homes and commercial buildings as well as excavations for water pipes can loosen the soil to a point where it can be easily eroded into the streams.

6   Construction of septic tanks for treatment of human waste is yet another activity that usually takes place in the early stages of a city's growth. If not properly constructed and located, they may pollute areas of the aquifer or groundwater. Without a sewage collection system, human wastes generally drain into groundwater, and this has caused outbreaks of cholera and typhoid.

7   During the second stage of urbanization, excavations are made for bigger houses and buildings. More soil is removed, and small pools of water are filled up. Soil erosion and sedimentation in the streams happens more quickly.

8   As the city expands, there will be an increase in surfaces that do not allow water to drain into the ground, resulting in a reduction of water reaching the groundwater. Because more water stays on the surface, other streams are overloaded, and some flooding results.

9   Another development during the second stage of city growth is the discharge of chemicals or insufficiently treated waste water into the area's streams. This pollutes the receiving streams, seriously affects human health, and often leads to the killing of aquatic life. Use of the area's water for recreation will be affected. The pollution also affects people living downstream from the city that is causing the pollution.

10   The third and final stage of urbanization is marked by nearly all of the original open soil being covered with buildings and streets. Much less water reaches the groundwater, and stream runoff is increased and speeded up.

11   With less water going underground, wells may have to be deepened to meet the needs of a larger population, or the city may have to reach beyond its own area to use water sources much further away.

12   The United States Environmental Protection Agency has identified a number of major sources of pollution to underground water in the United States. Most are related to urbanization. They include deep holes that are dug to "dispose" of hazardous wastes; accidental spills of these materials on city streets, factories, railroads, and airports; leaks from pipelines and storage tanks; abandoned water wells; and overuse of agricultural chemicals.

13   Pumping deeper and deeper for more and more water can also lead to a lowering of the surface of the land. In the United States, Houston, on the Texas coast, has a serious problem with land lowering. So much water has been taken from the ground that the land within a 64-kilometer radius of the city center has dropped almost three meters below its original elevation.

14   Mexico City, at more than 2134 meters above the sea, has a similar problem. This major city has sunk about 10.7 meters during the past seventy years into

the lake bed on which it has been built. The cause? Withdrawal of water from the aquifer below.

15   Mexican authorities have been attempting to meet the increasing demand for water by getting water from rivers more than 160 kilometers away from the capital. By the year 2000, Mexico City's population may be more than 30 million, and therefore have the world's greatest urban concentration and a major water-supply problem. It is interesting to note that from 1960 to 1976, the water supply to Mexico City was more than doubled, but the amount available per person declined. And, in 1982, only 15 percent of the residents in urban areas around Mexico City had piped water for their homes.

(Adapted from *The Courier*, January 1985, pp. 25–26.)

QUESTIONS

Now write your answers to the questions from the beginning of the reading.

1. What problem does the article describe?

_____

_____

2. How many stages in the growth of cities are identified?

_____

Now read the article more slowly and carefully and do the following activities.

COMPREHENSION QUESTIONS

Answer each of the following questions in one or two sentences. Try to use different words from the words you find in the reading. You may work in pairs if your instructor asks you to.

1. What general effects of the growth of cities were identified at the beginning of the reading?

_____

_____

2. What happens during the first stage of the growth of cities?

_____

_____

3. What effect or effects do the events of the first stage have on the supply of water?

_____

_____

4. What happens during the second stage of the growth of cities?

_____

_____

5. What effect or effects do the events of the second stage have on the supply of water?

_____

_____

6. What happens during the third stage of the growth of cities?

_____

_____

7. What effect or effects do the events of the third stage have on the supply of water?

_____

_____

8. What has happened to the land under both Houston, Texas, in the United States, and Mexico City, Mexico? Why?

_____

_____

9. How have cities in the past and in the present tried to increase their water supplies?

_____

_____

SUMMARY WRITING

Write a short summary of the reading (no more than ten sentences). When you are finished, work with a partner and compare your summaries. Decide whether each summary has all the necessary information or whether it contains too much or too little information. Finally, read your summaries to the class or exchange them with another pair of students and get their opinion on whether it contains the right amount of information.

VOCABULARY EXERCISE

Find the following words in the reading and write a definition of each word as it is used there.

1. transformed: _____

_____

2. vegetation: _____

_____

3. well: _____

_____

4. sedimentation: _____

_____

5. aquifer: _____

_____

6. soil erosion: _____

_____

7. downstream: _____

_____

8. elevation: _____

_____

APPLYING THE TEXT

In many places water for drinking and cooking is in very short supply. This may be because there simply is no water (as in a desert), because the available water is salt water, or because the available water is not clean. When water is limited, it is important to use as little as possible.

Working in small groups, list five ways that people in your community can save water or reduce the amount of water they use. When all the groups are finished, compare the lists in class and agree on the five best suggestions.

As a class, write a letter to the people in your community asking them to save water. Include your suggestions in the letter.

CHAPTER REVIEW

In this chapter you have read about water. Answer the following questions about the readings. Work alone and answer for yourself. Most of the questions do not have one correct answer; the answers are your opinion or are true for you. When you are finished, discuss your answers with your instructor and the rest of the class.

1. Which reading did you learn the most from? Why?

_____

_____

_____

2. Write five pieces of information that you learned from reading this chapter:

a. _____

_____

b. _____

_____

c. _____

_____

d. _____

_____

e. _____

_____

3. Which reading was the most interesting? Why?

_____

_____

4. Which reading was the easiest to read? Why?

_____

_____

5. Which reading was the most difficult to read? Why?

_____

_____

6. Did any reading have personal experience or opinion in it? Which one?

_____

7. Which reading had the most research in it?

_____

RESEARCH ACTIVITY

Working in groups, do some research on a topic related to water and prepare a report on it. Choose one of the following topics, or your instructor will assign a topic to you. Read at least five sources of information on the subject. Group members can collect information separately and then work together to combine and evaluate it.

Topic I: Desalinization

In many parts of the world, little fresh water is available but sea water is. Rather than try to find new sources of natural fresh water, some countries have tried to take the salt out of sea water, or desalinize it. This can be accomplished in several ways, but there are many problems associated with the process.

Your report might present the following information:

1. The need for fresh water
2. Introduction to different ways to desalinize sea water
3. How each method works and the good and bad points of each (with examples)
4. The best plan for the future

You may change this plan if the group members and your instructor agree on a different one.

Topic II: Pollution of Local Water Supplies

Is there any pollution of the water supplies in the area where you are studying? If there is enough information to read about such pollution, prepare a report on that problem. Pollution can come from industry (factories), from agriculture, and from human wastes.

Your report might include the following information:

1. How polluted local water supplies are
2. The sources of pollution
3. How each source is causing pollution
4. Possible solutions to the pollution problem

Topic III: Drought

Many parts of the world have experienced a temporary lack of rainfall. Such shortages cause droughts, or periods when water is in very short supply. Choose an area that is presently having a drought or one that had a drought recently. Read what you can about the drought and prepare your report. It might include the following information:

1. Where the drought is and how serious it is
2. What problems the people are having
3. Possible causes for the drought or events that are making it worse
4. What is being done to improve the problem

READING JOURNAL

List the outside reading you did while studying this chapter. (Include the title or type of material, length, topic or subject, and where you found the material.)

_____

_____

_____

Write a journal entry for this outside reading. Your instructor will want to look at your journal and may ask you to tell the rest of the class about something you read. In your journal you might answer the following questions. Or you can write about anything else you felt or learned as you were reading.

What was the most interesting thing you read? Why was it interesting?

What was the least interesting thing you read? Why was it not interesting?

What is one piece of information you learned about water from your outside reading?

Was the reading you did difficult or easy? Why do you think it was difficult or easy?

Do you have questions about water that you can find the answers to by reading? What are they? What can you read to find the answers?

Did you enjoy the outside reading you did while you studied this chapter? Why or why not?

INDEX

Animal(s)
  exotic, raising, 157–158
  rights, 172–176
  sharks, great white, 159–160, 161–162
  trainer, Gunther Gebel-Williams, 167–168
Application activity, 89, 90, 120, 196, 205, 211

Caras, Roger, "We Must Find Alternatives to Animals in Research," 176
Chapter review, 30, 60, 91, 121, 148, 180, 212
Chart completion, 57
Coble, C., "Fresh Water on the Earth's Surface," (with Rice, Walla, and Murray), 190–194
Coble, C., "Oceans of the World," (with Rice, Walla, and Murray), 199–203
Comparison, 75, 136, 169, 178
Completion, 21, 44, 134, 144, 163
Comprehension questions, 14, 48, 75, 87, 115, 204, 208
Contest, 45, 120
Credit cards, 85, 87
Crossword puzzle, 28, 90, 148

Debate, 106
Definitions, 196, 206

Education
  adult, 17–19
  basic, 7–8
  first days of school, 10–13
  schools in Japan, 24–25
Extending the text, 206

Fill-in-the-blank, 8, 40, 72, 100, 103, 110, 131, 158, 195
Food
  doufu. See Food, tofu
  history, 106–108
  tofu, 113–115

Giving advice, 82, 141
Group work
  being rich, 79
  getting rich, 77
  making suggestions, 16
  using credit cards, 88
Guessing, 146

Information
  checking, 22, 26
  evaluation, 14, 50
  focusing, 156
  gathering, 5, 37, 69, 97, 129, 186
  identification, 109, 117, 135, 141
  selection, 27
  using, 197
Interview, 164
Introduction, 3, 35, 67, 95, 127, 153, 185
"Is a Lab Rat's Fate More Important than a Child's?" (McCabe), 174

Long reading, 10, 17, 23, 41, 46, 50, 73, 80, 84, 101, 106, 112, 132, 138, 143, 159, 166, 172, 189, 198, 206

Marriage
  customs, 133–134, 143–144
  international, 133–134, 139–140
  records, 130–131

McCabe, Jane, "Is a Lab Rat's Fate More
    Important than a Child's?", 174
Money
    interest on, 84–85
    made from, 70–71
    obtaining, 74–75
    saving, 80–81
Murray, C., "Fresh Water on the Earth's
    Surface," (with Coble, Rice, and
    Walla), 190–194
Murray, C., "Oceans of the World," (with
    Coble, Rice, and Walla), 199–203
"Myth of the Monster, The" (Tennesen),
    161–162
Myths. *See* Newspapers, myths in

New information, 59, 77, 118, 164
Newspaper description, 58
Newspapers
    Al-Ahram (Egypt), 63
    Christian Science Monitor (USA), 55–56
    circulation, 51–52
    good qualities of, 52, 53–57
    myths in, 46–47
    Straits Times (Singapore), 54–55
Nutrition, 99–100

Origins, 109
Outside reading, 3, 36, 68, 96, 128, 155,
    186

Paraphrase, 110, 145
Photocopying, history of, 41–43
Problem solving, 23, 82, 89, 120

Reading journal, 32, 64, 93, 151, 183, 214
Reasons and opinions, 178
Report, preparing, 197
Research activity, 213
Restatement, 20
Rice, D., "Fresh Water on the Earth's
    Surface," (with Coble, Murray, and
    Walla), 190–194
Rice, D., "Oceans of the World," (with
    Coble, Murray, and Walla), 199–203
Rumors. *See* Newspapers, myths in

Short reading, 7, 38, 70, 98, 130, 157, 187
Soybean

appearance, 113
history, 113
makeup, 113–114
production, 114
uses, 113–114
Summary writing, 26, 44, 83, 103, 170, 204,
    210
Survey, 104

Television, history of, 38–39
Tennesen, Michael, "The Myth of the
    Monster," 161–162
Tofu. *See* Food, tofu

Vegetarianism, 101–103
Vocabulary
    exercise, 16, 22, 28, 45, 49, 58, 76, 83,
        88, 105, 111, 118, 136, 142, 147, 164,
        171, 211
    introduction, 3, 35, 67, 95, 127, 153

Walla, K., "Fresh Water on the Earth's
    Surface," (with Coble, Murray and
    Rice), 190–194
Walla, K., "Oceans of the World," (with
    Coble, Murray and Rice), 199–203
Water, fresh
    lakes and ponds, 193
    reservoirs, 190–192
    running water, 192–193
    standing water, 193
    water cycle, 190–192
Water, general information on, 187–188
Water, salt
    gases in, 201
    oceans, 199–200
    properties of, 200
    salts in, 200–201
    temperature, 201–203
Water and urbanization, 206–207
"We Must Find Alternatives to Animals in
    Research" (Caras), 176
Word forms, 59
Writing, 17, 28
Writing or speaking summary, 31, 63, 93,
    151, 182

Xerography. *See* Photocopying